Chambers

Pocket Guide to Music Forms & Styles

Also published by Chambers

Chambers Pocket Guide to Language of Music

Chambers
Pocket Guide to Music Forms & Styles

Wendy Munro

Chambers

British Library Cataloguing in Publication Data

Munro, Wendy
Pocket guide to music forms & styles.
— (Chambers pocket guides).
1. Music—Dictionaries
I. Title
780'.3'21 ML100

ISBN 0-550-18033-8

Typeset by Blackwood Pillans & Wilson Ltd.

Printed by Eyre & Spottiswoode Ltd, at Thanet Press, Margate

PREFACE

Music Forms & Styles is an A to Z of terms from baroque to rock, polyphonic to punk and fugue to funk. A sound knowledge of musical forms and styles is the key to understanding the whole field of music, and a special feature of this pocket guide is the inclusion of styles central to the development and interpretation of 20th-century popular music. But what exactly is a form and a style?

Form is the structure around which style is created. It is rather like building a house; after deciding on the basic size, shape and plan, a house may be built in an ornamental baroque style or perhaps in an angular modern style. The same happens in music. A sonata is formed in three main sections, each with a particular role to play, but a Mozart sonata from the classical period would sound quite different to a sonata composed by Hindemith in the 20th century. The difference here is a matter of style. However, this pocket guide is not written for the music specialist alone but for anyone who has even a passing interest in the subject and wants to know more.

The book is also easy to use. Each headword is in bold type, e.g. **fugue** or **aleatoric music**. For every heading I have tried to include dates, characteristic points of style, analysis of form, and composers who wrote that particular type of style with examples of actual works. Within the entries there may be other terms in bold type which indicates that you can look up more information under that particular word. Italics are used for titles of works and songs and nothing is abbreviated apart from R&B for rhythm and blues in the popular music entries. Normally, the headword is in the most generally accepted form, e.g. **musique concrète** (French) as opposed to the English form 'concrete music'. Similarly, the titles of works are mainly given in the language of their origin.

Music never ceases to be fascinating with new developments arising constantly. This book will keep you up-to-date with modern terminology but will also remind you of music of the past which, as Stravinsky said 'animates and informs the present'.

Wendy Munro

List of Abbreviations

Am.	American
Brit.	British
Czech.	Czechoslovakian
Eng.	English
Fr.	French
Gael.	Gaelic
Ger.	German
Gk.	Greek
Hung.	Hungarian
It.	Italian
Lat.	Latin
Pol.	Polish
Port.	Portuguese
Prov.	Provençal
Russ.	Russian
Sp.	Spanish

A

absolute music
The opposite of programme music, having no reference to any other art forms or emotions, e.g. literature, painting, etc. Most music is absolute, being written purely as music.

abstract music
Same as **absolute music**. However, *abstrakte musik*, as used by German writers, indicates dry and rather insensitive music.

a capella
See **cappella**.

acid rock
See **psychedelic rock**.

action song
Usually young children's song involving dramatic movement while singing.

act tune
A 17th- and 18th-century term to describe music between acts of plays. This music was often published independently. The modern term is *entr'acte*.

ad libitum or **ad lib** (Lat., 'at will')
This term indicates that the performer may, according to the context, either (a) alter the strict rhythm or tempo, (b) omit or include an instrumental or vocal part, (c) omit or include an entire passage, e.g. a **cadenza**, or (d) include a cadenza and play what and how he pleases. See also **improvisation**.

aeolian mode
One of a series of twelve modes, this one being based on A to A on white notes on piano. See **modes**.

agogic

In general, this term describes the natural musical expression one would use to play well, by varying the rate of movement, i.e. pausing, rubato, accenting, accelerando, etc.

air

This may describe either the melodic top part of a composition or a highly melodic entire composition, e.g. J.S. Bach's *Air on a G String*, now jazzed up and heard in a famous TV cigar advertisement of the 1970s and 1980s.

air with variations

A highly popular form since the 16th century in which a melody or subject is stated and is then played over several times with slight changes on each repetition with the original identity of the melody never being lost.

alalà

Spanish folk song in the **plainsong** mould. Usually in four-line verses with a melody highly decorated by the singer.

alberti bass

A broken chord moving accompaniment to a right hand melody characteristic of the classical period and most commonly found in keyboard music. It derives its name from Alberti, the Italian composer. Haydn and Mozart both used this formula.

alborada (Sp., 'morning song'), **aubade** (Fr.)

Characterised by a freedom of rhythm, this term is now applied to bagpipe and side-drum music popular in Galicia. Ravel and Rimsky-Korsakov also used this style in their music.

albumblatt (Ger., 'album leaf')

A 19th-century title given by composers like Wagner to short,

aleatoric music (Lat. *alea,* 'dice')

Music containing chance elements, i.e. where the composer leaves music in an indeterminate state. This 'random element' may be controlled by writing sections which can be played in any order, or where chance really is central to the composition. The concept of aleatoric music began with Charles Ives who influenced Cowell, the American experimentalist who devised 'elastic notations' which were musical fragments to be assembled by the performers. John Cage began using 'chance operations' in the early 1950s, his later music leaving a great deal to chance. Other composers include Stockhausen who composed *Klavierstück XI* (1956) which is written as an assortment of fragments spread over a large sheet of paper to be joined freely by the player. 'Mobile form', as practised by Berlioz, involved whole sections being changed around according to choice.

allemande

A term applied to two quite separate compositions but both originating in Germany. (1) A moderately slow dance movement often opening the baroque **suite** in 4/4 time. Usually in binary form each 'half' begins with a short note at the end of the bar. Highly decorated melodies and short note groupings are also features of this form. (2) A brisk dance in triple time, current in the late 18th and early 19th centuries. A prototype of the waltz.

ambient music

In the rock field this is a mid-70s style conceived by Brian Eno 'intended to induce calm and space to think', and to be a more sophisticated **muzak**. Influenced by John Cage, in writing music which could be easily listened to or ignored, this 'background music' incorporates synthesisers, life sounds, snatches of melodies and pleasing harmonies, all to wash over the listener. In art music composers include Erik Satie and Milhaud, whose furniture music, intended to be inconsequential, was playable both in public and at home.

ambrosian chant modes

A type of **plainsong** associated with Bishop St Ambrose of Milan at the end of the 4th century, who fixed upon four scales or modes to use for church composition. Using only the white notes on the piano, where the fifth dominates, and the root or bottom acts as a point of rest, the ambrosian modes are as follows:

D to D	with dominant A
E to E	with dominant B (later C)
F to F	with dominant C
G to G	with dominant D

Plainsong was established around these four modes. See also **gregorian modes**, which were developed later.

andaluz, andaluza (Sp.), **Aadalouse** (Fr.)

A term applied to several types of Spanish dance popular in Andalusia, e.g. fandango, malagueña and polo.

anglican chant

A type of harmonised melody used for psalm singing in the Church of England. A short melody is repeated to each verse of the text, with a 'reciting note', accommodating the varying number of syllables, appearing at the beginning of every line. Similar in principle to the gregorian chant.

anthem

Generally a short solemn vocal composition, derived from the Latin **motet** of the Roman Church, included in Church of England services, but music is not necessarily set to a liturgical text. The anthem may have solo parts and organ accompaniment.

antiphon (Gk.)

Plainsong setting of sacred words sung as responses in Roman Catholic and Greek Orthodox services. The term antiphonal derives from the practice of alternating performances between sets of singers stationed apart.

aquarelle (Fr., 'water colour')

A term sometimes applied to music of a delicate texture.

arabesque (Fr., Eng.), **arabeske** (Ger.)

A short piece or melodic figure which is highly decorated (like ornamental architecture in Arabic style). First written by Schumann and later by Debussy and others who entitled whole pieces in this style.

aria

An air or song for one or more voices now used exclusively of solo song in opera and oratorio. In the early 17th century the term was applied to structured more melodic vocal music in contrast to **recitative**. In the 18th century the form became clearer as a long vocal piece in three sections with the third merely repeating the first, and the second in a different key, more modulatory and offering variety of subject matter and mood. The third section was not usually written out, but indicated by the words *da capo*, thus the phrase *da capo aria*. It became a medium of vocal display in operas and many styles of arias were written, e.g. *aria cantabile, aria bravura, aria buffa* etc. Occasionally, this term may also be applied to instrumental pieces with song-like character.

arietta (It.), **ariette** (Fr.)
A little or light aria, i.e. short song or instrumental piece, often with the middle section omitted. See **aria**.

arioso (It., 'like an aria')
The term has various meanings. May be a more melodic, expressive **recitative** (much used by Bach and modern composers), a short, lyrical vocal solo, or an instrumental piece in vocal arioso style.

ars antiqua (Lat., 'old art')
A term coined in the 14th century to describe earlier medieval styles of music based on **plainsong** and **organum**.

ars nova (Lat., 'new art')
Breaking away from **ars antiqua** introducing duple time and much independence of part writing. It came to fruition in the Italian madrigal.

atonal music, atonalism
Not in any fixed key. A style which began with Debussy and Wagner who disguised the tonal centre of music with increasing modulation. Schönberg was the chief figure in this musical evolution, devising the twelve-note system of atonality. **Serialism** and **dodecaphonic** music also refer to this style. Atonal composers include Berg, Webern and Stockhausen. See also **note-row**.

aubade (Fr.)
See **alborada**.

augmentation
A lengthened statement of theme, usually by doubling time-values of notes. The opposite of **diminution**. Often used in **fugue**.

ayre
A melodic song for one or several voices in 17th-century England.

B

bagatelle (Fr., 'trifle')
A short light piece often for piano.

ballad
A traditional song telling a story with the same music repeated at each verse. It became a sentimental drawing room song in the late 19th and early 20th centuries.

ballade (Fr.)
Either, (1) a type of medieval French verse with refrain set to music, or (2) an instrumental romantic piece suggesting narrative, first pioneered by Chopin, e.g. his ballades for piano which were inspired by the Polish epic poems of Mickiewicz.

ballad opera
A type of opera popular in mid-18th-century Britain, featuring spoken dialogue interspersed with popular tunes of the day set to new words, e.g. John Gay's *The Beggar's Opera* (1728).

ballata
An Italian verse form of the 14th century, usually set to music with a refrain appearing at the beginning and end of stanzas.

ballet
A dance form of Italian origin incorporating drama, musical accompaniment and costumes. Established at the French Court in the 16th century, it led to the development of English **masque**, eventually evolving into an art form using orchestral music. Diaghilev (1872-1929) inspired composers such as Stravinsky and Ravel to write for the ballet and a revival led to scores from Vaughan Williams, Britten, etc. Choreographers even created ballets out of standard concert hall pieces. Now applied in Britain to any lengthy stage dancing with artistic purpose but in America the term is withdrawn for dances not based on 'classical' techniques.

ballett (Eng.), **balletto** (It.)
A vocal composition in several parts but **homophonic** in style. Prominent in England and Italy around 1600, and similar to the **madrigal** with a 'fa la' refrain. Lively and dance-like with symmetrical rhythm.

barber shop music
Originated in barber shops of the 16th-18th centuries when barbers or customers waiting in the shop picked up an instrument and made music. Now applied to amateur male quartets singing home-spun arrangements of sentimental songs.

barcarolle (Fr. from It.)
A boating song originally sung by Venetian gondoliers and now applied to any piece of music in swaying 6/8 or 12/8 rhythm, e.g. the barcarolle from the third act of Offenbach's *The Tales of Hoffmann*.

baroque
An architectural term of the 17th and early 18th centuries used to describe music of that time. Early baroque composers include Gabrieli and Monteverdi and late baroque composers include Scarlatti, Bach and Handel. The baroque style is typified by (1) figured bass or **basso continuo**, (2) the effect of harmony on melody and rhythm, e.g. when writing a **chaconne**, sequences of chords dominate, (3) balanced groups of bars in regular two, three or four beats, (4) use of clavichords, harpsichords and organs and (5) greater control over dynamic range. Ensembles were held together with keyboard accompaniment and suites and sonatas were written for this combination. The **concerto** was the characteristic orchestral form of the baroque era.

basse dance (Fr., 'low dance')
A French Court dance of the 15th and early 16th centuries. Of a serious nature where feet glided. Usually in two beats to a measure, although early examples have three beats. Instruments improvised around long notes featuring syncopations and rapid figurations. This dance was an ancestor of others like the stately **pavane**.

basso continuo (It.)
Also known as 'figured bass' and 'thorough bass'. A bass line central to 17th-18th century composition (i.e. **baroque** period).

basso ostinato

Usually marked with figures indicating harmonies to be played on keyboard or other chordal instrument. Actual bass notes (not harmonies) were also commonly sounded by 'cello etc. **Basso ostinato** or **ground bass** is a persistently repeated bass line figure or rhythm.

basso ostinato (It.)
Same as **ground bass**.

bebop, rebop or **bop**
A jazz style depending on modern harmony with dissonant chords influenced by musicians like Art Tatum and Lester Young. Rhythmically, bop was looser but more versatile and complex than earlier styles. The musicians accented measures on second and fourth instead of first and third beats or accented off the beats altogether. Harmonic rules were almost broken as more notes became acceptable and, therefore, a denser texture developed. New roles developed for instruments, i.e. the bass instrument shared the drum kit's time-keeping and progressed melodically while piano became lighter. Quintets of piano, bass, drums, reed instrument and trumpet became standard. References to known tunes were injected into solos based on another melody. With bop, jazz became recognised as a more serious art form for the first time. This style evolved into the 'modern' jazz of the 1950s and 1960s.

bel canto
Fine sustained singing in the Italian manner with emphasis on beauty of tone and agility.

berceuse (Fr.)
A lullaby or cradle song, but may be applied to quiet instrumental compositions with 6 beats to the bar suggestive of a lullaby, e.g. Chopin's *Berceuse* for piano.

bergamasque (Fr.), **bergamasca** (It.), **bergomask** (Eng.)
Originally a peasant dance from Bergamo, Italy. Also a tune and chord sequence from Bergamo widely used, e.g. as a **ground bass** in the 16th-17th centuries. In the 19th century it became a quick dance in 6/8 time similar to **tarantella**. Now used by composers without any special definition, e.g. Debussy's *Suite Bergamasque*.

binary form

In two sections. Definitions have varied as the form has progressed. In the 17th century the first section ended either on the tonic key or subdominant key, or else on an other related key, i.e. dominant or relative minor, which later became standard. The second section always ended in the tonic. Thus, the first section resulted in modulation to a related key and the second in modulating back to the tonic. In the 18th century the second section became longer than the first since it offered room for development. This form developed historically into **sonata form**, which is alternatively called *compound binary form*. See also **ternary form**.

black bottom

A form of **foxtrot**, popular at American and European dances for a short time in the 1920s.

block chords

Style of harmony where chords move in 'blocks', i.e. simultaneously, as opposed to contrapuntally where parts of chords move in different directions. This style was used by Debussy and by many jazz pianists.

blue beat

British name for **ska**.

blue grass

Originally country mountain music played on the fiddle, banjo and guitar, it merged with bass and mandolin in the 1920s and 1930s. Also influenced by **blues** and **jazz**. The skills of three-finger banjo-playing Earl Scruggs, Bill Monroe (tenor), and the three- and four-part harmonies (exemplified by the Stanley Brothers) were characteristics of the style. Blue grass also used old ballads, religious themes and no electric instruments. This novel combination brought back the topic of black suffering previously heard in the blues. Blue grass was superseded by **rock 'n' roll** in the 1950s, but groups like the Everly Brothers sang blue-grass harmonies and Elvis Presley's early songs had the eight-bar grouping blue-grass bass. The style is also evident in **rockabilly**.

blues

In the 16th century blues was an abbreviation of 'blue-devils' or melancholia. In the 19th-20th centuries blues refers to black folk music originating mainly in the deep south of the USA, describing a lonely, oppressed and hard existence. The blues flourished after the Civil War, developing from 'work songs' sung by negroes to relieve monotony and weariness in the cotton plantations. Lyrics were constructed out of three-line stanzas with second line repeating the first for emphasis often in iambic pentameter. Instrumentation was at first simple, with voice and perhaps acoustic guitar and harmonica, but became more complex as the style progressed. The melody was contained within twelve bars made up of three four-bar phrases. As blues developed other characteristics became evident, i.e. (1) flattening of thirds and sevenths (later fifths) in the diatonic scale (hence the expression 'blue-note') while accompaniment provided dissonance with traditional harmony; (2) 'breaks' appeared in the melody allowing performers to improvise, initially with phrases like 'oh laudy!' or 'oh baby!' and later with great instrumental embellishment. W.C. Handy (author of *The Memphis Blues* and *The St Louis Blues*) helped popularise this style of negro song throughout the country. Other great blues singers included Sophie Tucker, Bessie Smith, Ella Fitzgerald, Billie Holiday.

bolero
A Spanish dance in moderate triple time, often with triplet on second half of the first beat of the bar. Accompanied by castanets, but also including dancers' voices. Ravel's *Bolero* is not a true dancing bolero.

boogie-woogie
A piano jazz style developed out of guitar and piano blues traditions and the 'barrel-house' piano of southern US bars and brothels. This style was a rephrasing of the blues characterised by a bass line played eight beats to the bar. The technique has been described as 'trilling the treble and rolling the bass', i.e. flowing steady bass lines with the right hand playing grace notes, runs and trills. See also **stride**.

bossa nova (It., 'new bump')
A staccato, breathy style of Brazilian pop that plays down percussion and isolates the bass line, the vocal line and also a second independent melody line which may be played on guitar, piano or saxophone. Often the lyrics are bland, but the late Elis Regina performed some beautiful tone poems performed and

sung by Brazilian poet and playwright Vinicius de Moraes. Similar to **cool jazz.**

bourrée (Fr.), **bore** (It.), **borry, boree, borree, borre** (Eng.)
(1) A French dance in quick double time, starting in the third quarter of the bar and probably originating in the early 17th century. In the baroque suite it became an optional dance movement inserted between the **sarabande** and the **gigue**. Often two bourrées were written to form a contrasted pair as was done with the **minuet** and the **gavotte**. (2) Dance in triple time still popular in the French Auvergne.

brindisi (It.)
A toast or drinking song. Applied to a jovial song in which health is toasted. Such songs may also be found in operas, e.g. the brindisi from Donizetti's *Lucrezia Borgia* (1833).

burlesque (Fr.), **burla** (It.), **burleske** (Ger.)
Literally, 'jest'. Short piece of musical farce, lively and frolicsome in character. Also applied to lengthier compositions of a similar nature. Often associated with late 19th and early 20th century music hall turns.

C

cabaletta (It.)

Originally a simple **aria** with many repeats and much reiterated rhythm. Found in many of Rossini's operas. In the 19th century, the term was applied to the final section of elaborate operatic arias or duets. Cabaletta can also be a style of song in **rondo** form, often with variations on recurring passages.

cabaret

Inheriting its name from the French wine cellar or tavern, cabaret originated in Paris in 1881 growing out of the café-concert which was soon to become the French form of the music-hall. A more intellectual, intimate and self-consciously artistic form (although still essentially entertaining), cabaret was sparked by a literary society. Known as the 'Hydropathes', this group met weekly to perform works, e.g. poetry, a sung-lyric, a monologue or a short sketch. The lively gatherings, the impromptu stage and settings, the exchanging of ideas, the emphasis on the avant-garde and the development of the popular protest or satirical song as the main mode of expression were the initial ingredients of the cabaret in Paris. From there it travelled to Munich, Vienna and Berlin and was taken up by the Dadaists and the surrealists. During the Hitler years it provided a satirical haven for refugees and it has since developed new lives in *Monty Python* and *Beyond The Fringe*. The film *Cabaret* (1972) is only a distant relation of the original, conjuring up a rather seedy picture of strip joints, dark city streets and decadence.

cachucha

Spanish solo dance from Andalusia in 3/4 time. Similar to the bolero in rhythm.

cadence

A closing sentence or phrase in music through a progression of

chords. Although variation is possible the following conventional formulae for writing cadences have developed:
perfect cadence, dominant (chord V) to tonic (chord I), giving a finished feeling.
plagal cadence, subdominant (chord IV) to tonic (chord I), also a finished feeling sounding like 'amen'.
imperfect cadence, tonic or other chord to dominant (chord V). This progression feels unfinished, leading on to more music.
interrupted cadence, dominant (chord V) to submedient (chord VI), often sounding major to minor or minor to major, depending on the original key.

The above formulae are most commonly found in harmony text books, but others include:
feminine cadence, where the final chord arrives on a weaker beat than the previous chord.
Phrygian cadence, e.g. in the key of C major, the final chord being in E major. Popular in Bach's time.

cadenza (It., 'cadence')

In the 18th century the term described improvisation originally performed by opera singers before the final cadence of an aria. Instrumental soloists in concertos followed suite, with the convention of passing on the 6/4 chord, i.e. 2nd inversion of tonic (chord I). Improvisation would then take place with players expected to show off their virtuosity, develop previously stated themes and generally end with a long trill so that the orchestra could complete the cadence by progressing through the dominant and finally the tonic chords. In the classical concerto the cadenza appeared in the first movement. However, Mozart began the practice of writing out cadenzas, as did Beethoven and other later composers. Nowadays, therefore, the true improvised meaning of cadenza has disappeared.

calinda

A sensual South American negro dance imported by African slaves. Includes great use of percussion, especially drums. Delius wrote an orchestral piece called *La Calinda* in his opera, *Koanga* (1904).

calypso

A Trinidad song originating in the 18th century as a medium through which often censored news and views were heard.

Stanzas became longer and topics began to have lasting significance. Nowadays, this newspaper-like tradition continues. Basic melodies are simple, with syncopation and natural speech rhythms giving songs a lively style. At the turn of the century minor keys were favoured, but major keys are now more fashionable. Early instrumentation included sticks, drums, bottles, scrapers, etc. but today's version, **soca**, is more electronic. Music is still often associated with carnivals. Calypso spread to Britain and the USA in the late 1940s. One of the greatest exponents of this style was Calypso Rose.

cancan
High-kicking, lusty, Parisian dance of the late 19th century in quick 2/4 time. Used by Offenbach in *Orpheus in the Underworld* (1858). A hit for the 1970s two-tone band, *Bad Manners*, fronted by Buster Bloodvessel.

cancrizans
See **canon**.

canon
Polyphonic music in which the first statement of a melody is imitated by one or more parts, each entering before the previous one has finished, thus overlapping results. Types include:
canon at the unison, imitation at the same pitch as the first voice.
canon at the fifth, imitation a fifth higher than the first voice.
canon two in one, simple canon in two parts.
canon four in two (double canon), combination of two two-part canons.
strict canon, exact imitation.
free canon, modified imitation.
perpetual or *infinite canon,* whole canon repeating (popularly known as a **round**).
crab canon or *cancrizans,* the imitating part written backwards and upside down.
canon by augmentation, diminution, inversion, etc., canons where imitating voices are treated in any of these ways.

cantata (It.)
A vocal piece, unlike counterpart sonata, which is instrumental. In the early 17th century it was a secular piece similar to opera (i.e. including **recitative** and **arias**), but for concerts rather than full stage performance. Later it was extended and elaborated to

include the setting of religious texts. Bach adopted the German introduction of Lutheran **chorale** into cantata which was scored for soloists, chorus and orchestra. Since the late 18th century the term has been applied to sacred or secular works, with or without soloists, accompanied by orchestra. The cantata is similar to the **oratorio** but less extended.

cante flamenco
See **flamenco**.

canti carnascialeschi (It., 'carnival songs')
Similar to early **madrigals** of a popular nature sung in processions at festivals in the 15th and 16th centuries. The tune was often sung in the tenor with words that were sometimes improper and with several verses to the same music. The songs were opposed by Savonarola, a religious leader, who wrote the *Laudi Spirituali* in their place.

canticle
A hymn with biblical words, but not taken from psalms used in Christian liturgy. The term may also be applied to a concert piece involving a religious text.

cantiga
A Spanish or Portuguese folk song. At the end of the 13th century Alfonso X of Léon and Castile made a collection of examples of the cantiga showing the influence of the troubadours.

cantilena (It.)
Nowadays, a smooth, flowing melodic line. The term has been used in the past to describe either the main uppermost tune in choral music or a type of solfeggio.

cantillation
Unaccompanied chanting in **plainsong** style with a free rhythm, especially in Jewish liturgical music.

canzona or **canzone** (It., 'song' or 'songs')
Generally applied to a vocal piece or an instrumental piece modelled on vocal form. In medieval times it was a polyphonic musical setting of an Italian secular poem. From the 16th to the early 19th centuries it was a short instrumental piece developed from the contemporary French **chanson**, but less polyphonic

than **ricercar**. In opera, the term described a simple song unlike the elaborate **aria.**

canzonetta (It.), **canzonet** (Eng.)
A short and secular light song for one or more voices with or without instrumental accompaniment. In the 16th century the form was usually AABCC.

cappella (It., 'chapel') or **a cappella** (It., 'in the chapel style')
Unaccompanied choral music. In the 17th century the term was similar to *ripieno* (It., 'all performing').

capriccio (It.), **caprice** (Fr.)
A term applied to various light pieces, particularly to lively fugal style works of the 17th century. It may also be a technical study or rhapsody.

carol, noël (Fr.), **Weinachtslied** (Ger.)
Today, a Christmas song singable by untrained vocalists, but in medieval English a carol was any song with a refrain.

catch
An entertaining type of **round** sometimes with coarse words popularised in the 17th century, e.g. by Purcell.

cavatina (It.)
An 18th-century term for the **arioso** section occurring in **recitative**. This was originally an operatic song in regular form, unlike the *da capo aria*, in three sections.. Hence, the rather slow song-like instrumental movement, e.g. the famous *Cavatina* by the German composer, Raff (1822-82), used in the film *The Deer Hunter*, but originally written for violin and piano.

cebell
A quick **gavotte**-like dance in 17th-century England. Purcell, and others adopted this style for harpsichord pieces, a characteristic of which was a contrasting of high and low passages.

ceilidh
A Scottish highland social gathering largely consisting of songs and instrumental music for dancing, lasting the whole night long.

chacha
A Cuban dance dating from the 1950s, later introduced to the USA and further afield. This developed from the earlier 'mambo' dance and is still popular in ballrooms today.

chaconne (Fr.), **ciaccona** (It.)
A stately dance in slow triple time in which a theme (usually a bass line) or harmonic pattern is varied. The chaconne may be vocal or instrumental and was especially popular in 17th-century opera and keyboard music. Similar to the **passacaglia**.

chamber music, **musique de chambre** (Fr.), **kammermusik** (Ger.), **musica da camera** (It.)
Music intended for a room as distinct from a large hall, theatre, etc. Originally, instrumental as well as vocal works were included, but nowadays the term generally applies to instrumental music of a more intimate nature with a limited number of performers. Characteristic chamber music styles include: (1) the **fantasia** or **ricercar** for viols in the 16th and early 17th centuries; (2) the trio sonata for two violins and bass with organ or harpsichord in the 17th- and early 18th-centuries, and (3) the string quartets for two violins, viola and 'cello from the late 18th-century to the 20th-century. However, many other combinations are possible.

chamber opera
A reduced opera suitable for a smaller venue.

chamber sonata
See **sonata da camera**.

chanson
A song for one or several voices sometimes with instruments current in the 14th-18th centuries in France and Italy. The chanson was similar to the early **madrigal** with the tune in the tenor part often being a folk melody. However, the modern French word for solo song with piano accompaniment, etc. is *melodie*. This term may also describe an instrumental piece of vocal character. A *chanson de gueste* was a type of heroic verse set to music current in the 11th- and 12th-centuries.

characteristic piece, charakterstück (Ger.)
Usually a short piece, often for piano, representing a mood or place, etc.

Charleston
A type of **fox-trot**, originally popular with negroes from the southern states of the USA. Played in 4/4 time, the characteristic rhythm of this dance divides the bar into a dotted crotchet followed by a quaver tied to a minim.

chorale (Eng. phonetic spelling of Ger. *choral*)
A metrical hymn tune of the Lutheran church. In the 16th century materials used for chorales included adaptations of Roman Catholic Church Latin hymns, secular songs and original hymns, e.g. *Ein feste Burg* used by Bach. Melodies began to show great rhythmical freedom but in the 18th century the shape became more symmetrical. A *chorale cantata* makes use of the text and melody of a Lutheran hymn or chorale. A *chorale prelude* is usually organ music based on a hymn tune with the melody being used as a basis of a **fugue**, etc. A *chorale fantasia* or *fantasy* describes a chorale melody, freely treated usually on the organ.

chromatic
This term describes the intervals or notes outside the **diatonic** scale (ie the major or minor scale). Chromatic scales are made up entirely of semitones, whereas the diatonic scales (e.g. C major) consist of tones and semitones. Therefore, music described as chromatic, or as having chromatic harmonies, involves departure from the prevailing diatonic scales, thus usually demanding modulation.

classical music
A constantly mis-used word, this term actually refers to 18th- and early 19th-century music embracing the classical **concerto**, **symphony** and string quartet. The classical style embodies clarity, balance, order and restraint and it is not concerned with the expressions of individual emotion like **romantic music**. However, to the uninitiated who say 'I hate classical music', this term means all music which is not **pop**. Generally accepted classical composers include Mozart and Haydn.

close harmony
Harmony in which chord parts lie close together. Opposite of **open harmony**.

coda (It., 'tail-piece')
The end passage of a piece or a movement. In **sonata form** a

short coda is added to the end of the recapitulation, but Beethoven's codas were much extended. In **canon** the coda is short with no strict imitation to arrive at a convincing cadence. In **fugue** the coda is often based on a pedal point reaching a conclusion. See also **codetta**.

codetta (It., diminutive of **coda**, 'little tail')
(1) A rounding off passage of a section of a composition or (2) an extension of a **fugue** subject in order to delay the next entry.

collage
A synthesis of musical styles, e.g. *Sergeant Pepper* by The Beatles, which involves Indian Raga, **tin pan alley** and other strange sounds. Charles Ives (1874-1954) wrote and experimented in this style. See also **underground rock**.

coloratura (It.)
Agile and florid vocal music.

comic opera
See **opera**.

community singing
Public singing at meetings, parties, etc. Therefore, community songs were written for such occasions.

compound binary
This is the same as **sonata form**, developing historically from **binary form**.

concertant (Fr.), **concertante** (It.)
As an adjective, the term describes music for an orchestra, or for two or more instruments in which one or more solo parts are prominent. As a noun, 'concertante' is synonymous with *sinfonia concertante*, i.e. a work for solo instrument(s) and orchestra having a form closer to a **symphony** than **concerto**.

concerto (It.), **concert** (Fr.), **konzert** (Ger.)
This term has had several definitions. Originally, the concerto was a work for one or more voices with instrumental accompaniment often incorporating **figured-bass**. In the 17th and early 18th-centuries it became known as a contrasting work for several instruments with figured-bass. This definition is also

used by modern composers. From the early 18th-century the *solo concerto* became the normal type, i.e. a concerto for a solo instrument and orchestra, and by Mozart's time figured-bass became extinct, although the piano or harpsichord still played with the orchestra even in keyboard concertos. This form was similar to the operatic aria with contrasts between the full orchestra and solo sections. Room for improvised instrumental display was made at the cadence before the final ritornello (full orchestra). See also **cadenza**.

concerto grosso (It., 'great concerto')
In the 17th- and 18th-centuries this was an orchestral work involving contrasts between all the performers (*ripieno*) and a smaller group (*concertino*), each with its own **continuo**, unlike the modern definition of concerto where one performer provides the contrast. This term is also used to describe 20th-century works based on 17th- and 18th-century models.

concert overture
A 19th-century form describing an orchestral piece similar to an overture or opera, etc. but only intended for the concert room, e.g. *The Hebrides* by Mendelssohn.

concertstück (Ger.) or **concert piece**
A briefer and less formal **concerto** without breaks between the sections but involving contrasting sections between soloist and full orchestra. A romantic musical term.

conga
A Caribbean dance in which people form a long winding line.

continuo (It.)
An abbreviation of **basso continuo**.

contredanse (Fr.), **kontretanz** (Ger.), **contradanza** (It.)
These words are corruptions of 'country dance' originating in England and popular in 18th-century France and Germany. A lively dance cultivated by Mozart and Beethoven.

counterpoint
The combination of two or more melodies or parts to make musical sense. Therefore, one melody (A) is said to be in counterpoint to melody (B) etc. Many types exist: *invertible*

counterpoint describes parts which can be interchanged; *double counterpoint* is invertible counterpoint between two parts. In the 16th century *strict counterpoint* insisted upon certain rules and *free counterpoint* denoted contrapuntal writing not bound by such tight formulae.

country music
Music of many styles, e.g. **hillbilly** and **country 'n' western**, but all styles deal with everyday problems to which man can relate. Country music began with ballad songs originally brought to the USA by British white settlers taking root in places like Tennessee and Kentucky. Words were adapted as time progressed to describe local characters, happenings and culture giving the music a live feel. Instrumentation originally was primitive, e.g. a banjo (simply hide stretched over a gourd), a fiddle and a single-stringed bow.

country 'n' western
This is commercial **hillbilly** music inspired by Jimmy Rodgers who moved west, donned the cowboy regalia and recorded many western-orientated songs. The 'singing cowboys' thus became fashionable (e.g. Gene Autry and Roy Rogers) but the rough hillbilly image was erased to have a wider appeal. The country music centre shifted away from Kentucky and Tennessee to the radio stations of the South West. However, Nashville was later to become the home of this music again. Exponents of the country 'n' western style include Dolly Parton, Tammy Wynette and George Hamilton IV.

couplet
In the early French **rondo**, episodes were called couplets, especially when written by Couperin.

courante (Fr.), **coranto, corrente** (It.)
Short for *danse courante* or 'running dance'. This was a dance in triple time with a standard position in the **baroque suite**, following the **allemande**.

crab canon
See **canon**.

cracovienne (Fr.)
See **krakowiak**.

cradle song
Same as **berceuse**.

crooning
A style of singing popular in the 1930s and 40s which was excessively sentimental. The singer performed with a microphone and back-up dance band. Exponents included Rudy Vallée and later Bing Crosby.

csárdás (Hung.)
A Hungarian dance in two contrasting and alternating sections. Firstly, the slow and melancholy *lassú* and secondly, the quick and lively *friss*.

curtain music
Same as **act tune**.

cyclic form
This term is applied to an extended work with a sense of unity (usually thematic) linking sections or movements. In the 15th-century *cyclic masses* were written. In 16th- and 17th-century *dance suites* there is also thematic connection. However, this form was particularly developed by Romantic composers, e.g. the song cycle entitled *Woman's Love and Life* by Schumann (1810-1856).

D

dance band

An instrumental group established in the 1930s for strict tempo dancing consisting of three sections (1) a reed section with saxophones, some doubling as clarinets, (2) brass section with trumpets and trombones and (3) rhythm section including piano, drums, guitar and a pizzicato double bass. From the 1950s the pop group became more fashionable.

development

A section of a movement where thematic material is developed, e.g. expanded, combined, or inverted. In **sonata form** the development section is performed after the initial statements of themes and before the recapitulation.

diatonic

Opposite of **chromatic**, i.e. keeping exactly to the notes of the chosen key. In C major, for example, CDEFGABC are all diatonic notes. Any other notes, e.g. F sharp, would be accidental and therefore, chromatic. In minor keys, the sharpened sixth and seventh are considered diatonic since they are in such common use. Therefore, a *diatonic chord* only uses notes proper to the key, and *diatonic harmony* employs predominantly diatonic chords.

diminution

A shortened statement of a theme or melody usually created by halving the time-values of notes. This device is often used in **fugue** and is the opposite of **augmentation**.

discant

A development of **organum**, a type of medieval part-writing or early **counterpoint**.

disco

A sound which is a blend of musical styles with electronic techniques and, above all, a steady danceable beat usually in 4/4 time carried by drums or bass. Requiring the use of bigger sound systems, the disco sound was aimed at the dance floor, and resulted in the development of multi-tracking skills in combination with the full symphony orchestra. Whistles, sirens and other live sounds are often used for effect and the synthesiser enables electronic waves to change frequency, never going below 70 beats a minute (normal pulse rate) so that the music is constantly stimulating. The *Philadelphia disco sound* is associated with black soul played in rich symphonic sounds. The German sound features strong violin, synthesisers and whistles. The Latin beat refers to disco versions of the **cha-cha, tango**, etc. Lighting, mirrors and shiny surfaces are also central to the disco atmosphere. Disco singers include Diana Ross, Donna Summer and Sister Sledge. Disco songs include *He's the Greatest Dancer, Jive Talkin'* etc. All these songs are light and bouncy with lyrics about love, dancing and Saturday nights on the town.

divertimento

This is chiefly an 18th-century term for an entertaining suite with movements for a chamber ensemble or orchestra. Mozart composed many divertimentos and the title has been used by other 20th-century composers, e.g. by Bartok (1881-1945) in his *Divertimento* for strings.

dixieland

A style of **jazz** playing originating in New Orleans in the pre-1914 era. Simple, unsentimental and obviously syncopated, this style was performed by small groups. See **jazz**.

dodecaphonic or **dodecuple**

These terms refer to the *twelve-note system*. See **serial music**.

doo-wap

A style originating in New York as a spin-off from black R&B records. The doo-wap group usually consisted of four or more singers congregating on street corners singing **a capella** (i.e. without instrumentation). Basic chords I, II, V and VI were used and lyrics were about young love. Bass singers had an intricate part with a high falsetto on top. Harmonies were close-knit and phrases like *shoo-bop-sha-la-la, shoo-be-doo*, etc were characteristic of the style.

dumka (Russ. and Czech.)
A Slavonic term for a folk ballad or lament in which slow and fast tempos alternate. The term was also used by Dvorák.

dump or **dompe**
In the 16th and 17th centuries this musical and literary term denoted an elegy or lament and examples are often entitled with the person's name. All works in this style are instrumental and constructed over a **ground bass**.

E

entr'acte (Fr.)
Modern term for **act tune**.

entrée (Fr.)
This term is mainly used in 17th-century French music and has several meanings. It may be an introductory piece of instrumental music in opera or ballet or it may be a completely independent piece of instrumental music but similar in character to the previous definition. The term may also describe a self-contained section of a ballet or opera equivalent to a scene or act.

entry
In the 17th century the term described a **prelude**. In a **fugue**, however, an entry is an appearance or entrance of a theme at any point in the work, not necessarily just at the beginning.

episode
A section in instrumental music usually of a more subordinate nature but principally appearing in **rondo** as a contrasting and separating section between entries of the main theme, and in **fugue** as a section occurring between entries of a subject and providing a link often modulating to a related key.

episodical form
Same as **rondo form**.

equale (old It., plural *equali*; modern It., *eguale* 'equal')
In the 18th and 19th centuries the term described short pieces played in Austria at funerals, usually for trombone quartet. Beethoven composed a set of three pieces in this style.

estampie (Fr.) or **estampia** (Prov.)
A 13th- and 14th-century dance form in several sections (*puncta*), having a first ending (*ouvert*), and a second ending (*clos*). This form is associated with the Troubadours.

étude (Fr., 'study')
Any instrumental piece to improve or demonstrate certain technical points. In the 19th century the development of the new piano technique brought about many new books of études. A characteristic of this style is the appearance of a technical exercise with a motif which is developed, as is the exercise. However, many have much artistic merit (e.g. the études of Chopin).

exposition
Generally, this is a first statement of musical material on which the movement or piece is based. In **sonata form**, it is a repeated section in which main themes are first stated before moving on to the **development**. In **fugue**, it is the initial statement of the subject of all the voices in turn. When each voice has been heard, then the exposition is concluded.

expressionism
A term borrowed from painting and applied to other art forms implying a reaction against **impressionism**. It was first applied to the paintings of Kandinsky and others in 1910-11 and thereafter to the works of Schönberg and his pupils. Often identified with the Freudian unconscious, expressionism results from a need to be often violently personal and in order to achieve this there is a rejection in expressionist music of traditional forms, techniques and language. The term is normally used to describe Schönberg's atonal pre-serial music, e.g. *Erwartung* and *Pierrot Lunaire*.

extemporisation
Same as **improvisation**.

extravaganza (Anglicised version of It. *stravaganza*)
Stage entertainment of a farcical nature with music in 19th-century England, often with performance of new words to old and well-known tunes.

F

faburden (Eng.), **fauxbourdon** (Fr.), **falsobordone** (It.)

These terms literally mean 'false drone'. Originally, in 15th-century church music, the terms described a method of improvising two-part parallel harmony to a **plainsong** melody above. This term was later applied to a simple four-part harmonisation of plainsong. However, there are now two definitions in modern usage: (1) a harmonisation of a hymn in four parts with the tune in the tenor, (2) a treble part (or descant) sung above a hymn tune.

fado (Port.)

A Portuguese folk song in **binary form** with four beats to the bar. The fado may be fast or slow and is accompanied by guitar.

fa-la

A popular 16th- and early 17th-century part song known as **ballett** (Eng.) or **balletto** (It.) with the refrain or burden using the syllables 'fa la la'.

fandango

A Spanish dance in 3/4 or 6/8 time of lively character. Probably of South American origin, this dance is accompanied by the guitar and castanets with strains sung by the performers. Characteristics of the style are sudden stops or freezes when dancers stand motionless, and also increases in speed.

fanfare

A flourish for trumpets or for other instruments emulating trumpets, usually proclaiming a great event or acting as an introduction. Some fanfares are used in extended compositions. *Fanfare* (French) is a brass band.

fantasy (Eng.), **fantaisie** (Fr.), **fantasia** (It.), **fantasie** (Ger.)
This term has many meanings, but generally, it is a composition in which the composer follows his imagination or 'fancy' rather than set rules. In the 16th- and 17th-centuries the term was applied to a contrapuntal piece in several sections where a theme was developed freely by strings or keyboard. The term later described an improvisatory work for lute or keyboard or an extended work freer in form than a traditional sonata. It could also describe a work based on an existing theme or themes and was synonymous with the **development** section, e.g. in **sonata form** which was written as *free fantasia*. In the 19th century the term described a mood or character piece in the **romantic** era, e.g. Schumann's *Fantasie-Stücke* for piano.

farandole (Fr.)
A lively street dance of Provence in 6/8 time accompanied by players on pipe and tabor who precede the dancers in a long chain holding hands.

figure
A short musical phrase achieving distinction through repetition. It is too short to be a theme.

figured bass
A 17th- and 18th-century kind of continuo bass still practised in musical training today. See **basso continuo**.

finale (It., 'final')
In English there are two meanings. First, it may be the last movement of a work in several movements. In the 18th century the finale was brisk and bright, but Beethoven developed this, allowing more freedom for other composers. Second, it may be the concluding section of an act of an opera, employing several singers and often a chorus. This section was subdivided into smaller sections with contrasting tempos and keys.

first movement form
See **sonata form**.

flamenco or **cante flamenco** (Sp.)
A type of Spanish song from Andalusia with guitar accompaniment and dance. There are various sub-species named after other districts, e.g. *Malagueña, Sevillana*. The

flamenco is a lighter version of the sadder cante **hondo**. The flamenco style in guitar playing indicates quite a different technique with a change of fingering and much more forcefulness than one expects of the 'classical style'.

flamenco hondo (Sp.)
See **hondo**.

folk music
This term generally implies popular song or music ascribed to no particular composer preserved by oral tradition between generations. Therefore, folk music is likely to exist in several versions, but internationally there are similarities, e.g. the use of **modes**. In the 19th century folk music was identified with nationalist sentiment, with composers imitating characteristics of styles. In 20th-century popular music, Woodie Guthrie inherited the tradition and spirit of folk music using popular melodies as a vehicle for protest or news. This eventually developed into a large movement in the 1960s. See also **protest music** and **country music**.

foxtrot
A dance in duple time which may be slow or fast and is similar to **ragtime**. Originally this was a negro dance which became popular about 1912 and thereafter spread around the world.

free counterpoint
See **counterpoint**.

free fantasia
This term sometimes is applied to the **development** section of a movement, e.g. in **sonata form**.

frottola (It., 'little mixture')
A forerunner of the **madrigal**. The frottola was a popular strophic song flourishing around 1500 and particularly heard in Italian aristocratic circles.

fuga
This is both a Latin and Italian term. In Latin, it describes a **canon** in the 15th and 16th centuries. In Italian, the term means **fugue**.

fugato (It., 'fugued')
The term describes a section of a composition which is treated in fugal style, although the whole composition is not a **fugue**.

fughetta (It.)
A short **fugue**.

fugue
A contrapuntal composition for two or more voices or parts built around a *subject* which is introduced and imitated by each voice in turn and which reappears frequently during the composition. These entries of parts have specific roles to play. The first entry is in the tonic key and is called the subject. The second entry in the dominant, usually starting a fifth above or a fourth below, is called the *answer*. If there are more entries, they are often delayed for a few bars by a **codetta**, but continue, alternately, as above. If the answer exactly reproduces the subject a fifth above, etc. then this is called a *real answer* and the fugue a *real fugue*. If the answer is slightly modified, then it is a *tonal answer* and thus the fugue is a *tonal fugue*. An entry having announced the subject or answer follows on to a *countersubject* (another reappearing thematic element) heard simultaneously with the entry of the next voice. When all the voices have been heard the **exposition** is complete. However, occasionally in the initial entries there appears an extra voice, known as a *redundant* entry. Thereafter, the fugue consists of further entries of the subject, sometimes in related keys and sometimes presented and treated by **augmentation, diminution,** inversion, **stretto**, etc. A *double-fugue* is one in which a second independent subject appears combined with the first subject and similarly *triple fugue* and *quadruple fugue*. The great master of fugue was J.S. Bach.

funk
A euphemistic Black term for music suggesting sex and a simple lifestyle. With a raunchy rhythm, funk began in New Orleans with pianists creating new left-hand beats (called 'funky') and with bass players experimenting with the timing between their beats and the drum-beat. In the late 1960s and 1970s James Brown pursued funk especially for dancers. The style consisted of looser song structures, the percussive use of all instruments to evoke the rediscovery of African roots among American Blacks, punchy but fractured bass-lines, choked rhythm guitar, brass and lyrics which were repetitive with exhortations. Hits of James

Brown included *Hot* (1975) and *Body Heat* (1976). Other funk songs were Lee Dorsey's *Everything I Do Gonh Be Funky (From Now On)* (1969), and Funkadelic's *One Nation Under a Groove* (1978). The bass-slapping technique is a feature of today's funk bands which include the American Trouble Funk.

furiant (Czech.)
A quick Czech dance with syncopated rhythms.

furniture music
A 20th-century concept of serious music existing and being performed outside the concert hall, and having no pressure on the listener to pay attention. In 1920 Erik Satie and Milhaud created such a style by combining snippets of **pop** and operatic tunes of the day. Intended to be played during an intermission of a surrealistic play performed in an art gallery, one could listen or not listen to the music while inspecting the paintings. This style is a forerunner of Brian Eno's **ambient music** and also **muzak**.

futurism
A 20th-century movement started in 1911 by the Italian writer Marinetti and composer Rossolo, consisting of a revolution of music through the *Art of Noises*. Noise instruments, e.g. whistlers, exploders, etc. were used in composition to reflect the mechanical world around us. Rossolo thought the modern orchestra should have six groups of noisemakers accompanied by screams, snoring and animal voices, etc. Later other composers like Varèse wrote whole pieces in this style and *noise music* was accepted, e.g. *Ionisation* by Varèse, written in 1933. John Cage was a frontrunner in the development of noise pieces after World War II. He devised the *prepared piano* i.e. a piano with objects added to the string at various distances from the damper point to create new sounds.

G

galant

See **style galant**.

galliard (Eng.), **gaillarde** (Fr.), **gagliarda** (It.)

A lively dance originating in 15th-century Italy and usually in 3/2 time. From the 16th century the galliard was used in striking contrast to the slower **pavane** which it followed, often sharing the same musical material. The galliard involves quick and complex steps.

galop

A 19th-century popular quick round dance in 2/4 time. Originating in Germany, a characteristic of this style was a change of step or hop at the end of every half-phrase. It later ceased to be danced independently and became part of a set of the **quadrille**.

gavotte

An old French dance in fairly fast 4/4 time, usually beginning on the 3rd beat of the bar. Occasionally, it may be part of the Baroque Suite. However, it became popular with Lully's use of the gavotte in ballets and operas in the 17th century. Where two gavottes occur together, the 2nd is often in the form of a **musette**. The gavotte has been revived in modern times, e.g. by Prokofiev.

gebrauchmusik (Ger.) or **utility music**

This term was applied in Germany in the 1920s to the music of Hindemith, Weill and others who were influenced by Brecht and believed that the Arts should always retain a contact with the masses and that they should be directed to a social or educational purpose. The music should utilise idioms from everyday life and the composers were much against the 'Art for Art's sake' philosophy. Hindemith wrote music for both amateurs and professionals and Kurt Weill's *Der Jasager* is an example of the style.

gigue, giga (It.) also **jig**

Originally, this was a lively rustic dance first appearing in the 16th-century work of English virginal and lute composers, and spreading to the continent in the mid-17th century. In the late 17th and early 18th centuries the dance became standardised as having a 6/8 rhythm and when the **suite** developed, the gigue appeared last in the four dances following the **allemande**, **courante** and **sarabande**. The gigue was generally in **binary form** and there were by this stage, two main types: (1) a simple gigue of straight forward character and (2) a more elaborate gigue with fugal imitation and the subject inverted in the second section.

glam rock or **glitter rock**

A flamboyant 1970s rock movement involving David Bowie, Gary Glitter, Elton John, Roxy Music and Rod Stewart, all performing music of a simple superficial nature aimed at the teenage market. Flared trousers, make-up, satin suits and lots of glitter made up the image, and other groups like Mud, Sweet, T. Rex and The Bay City Rollers made their names by stepping on the bandwagon. The material was mainly composed by 1960s songwriters. Hit singles from the Glam Rock era included T. Rex's *Get it On*, and Elton John's *Rocket Man*.

glee

An unaccompanied short part-song in short movements for male voices, moving in block chords, i.e. it is not contrapuntal. The glee was popular in England in the 18th and early 19th centuries.

gondola song

This is a **barcarolle**, supposedly sung by the Venetian gondoliers and is usually in 6/8 or other compound time. The title *Gondola Song* has sometimes been applied to other instrumental compositions of a swaying nature, e.g. three of Mendelssohn's *Songs Without Words* for piano.

granadina (Sp.)

A kind of fandango from Granada similar to the **malagueña.**

grand opera

Originally a French 19th-century term to distinguish between operas with music throughout and *opéra-comique* which involves dialogue. However, it is now a general term for lavish scale performances and the considered difference to laymen between serious **opera** and **operetta**.

gregorian chant

A type of **plainsong** associated with Pope Gregory I at the end of the 6th century. Gregory added four more scales, or modes, to the **ambrosian** scales and developed a more consistent use of a dominant or reciting note. This chant still survives today in the Roman Catholic Church, consisting of a single unaccompanied line of vocal melody in free rhythm, i.e. with no regular bar lengths, since it has its own system of notation. See **gregorian modes** below.

gregorian modes

Pope Gregory I added to the **ambrosian modes** (which he called Authentic Modes) to allow greater variety. He added four *Plagal Modes* which were simply an extension of the same modes taken in another compass. The whole system of gregorian modes is as follows:

Mode I	D—D with Dominant A
Mode II	A—A with Dominant F
Mode III	E—E with Dominant C
Mode IV	B—B with Dominant A
Mode V	F—F with Dominant C
Mode VI	C—C with Dominant A
Mode VII	G—G with Dominant D
Mode VIII	D—D with Dominant C

ground bass or **basso ostinato** (It.)

A constantly repeated bass-line or pattern throughout a composition providing a foundation for varied melodic treatment, e.g. harmonic or contrapuntal. In the 17th and early 18th centuries the ground bass was much developed to attain unity and symmetry in music, as opposed to the **polyphonic** music of the 16th century. Improvisation above the ground bass was also common, and many forms are related, e.g. the **chaconne** and **passacaglia**. A famous example of ground bass is *When I am Laid in Earth* from the opera *Dido and Aeneas*, by Purcell.

gymel or **gimel** (Lat., *cantus gemellus* 'twin song')
In the 15th century the term described a characteristically English style of singing in two parts in parallel intervals of thirds and sixths. However, in the 14th- and early 15th-centuries the term described two-part singing, as above, but moving independently of a main tune below. It may also, as found in 16th-century choral music, simply mean 'divided'.

H

habanera (Sp.)

A slow Cuban dance (from Havana) which became popular in Spain in the 19th-century. It was usually written in 2/4 time with a characteristic syncopated rhythm. Various composers have used the style, e.g. Bizet in the opera *Carmen*.

halling

A moderately fast and popular Norwegian dance generally in 2/4 time. Performed by men, this dance involves dramatic action, e.g. wild leaps in the air, somersaults and kicking.

hard bop

A dynamic New York Jazz style reacting against *Cool Jazz*, based on relaxed rhythms.

heavy metal

This style started as *Heavy Rock*, with performers like Hendrix whose music was heavily amplified, with the guitar enhanced by feedback or wah-wah effects. The playing was loud and fast and *Purple Haze*, by Hendrix and *Born to be Wild* were forerunner songs out of which the style was to grow. Heavy riffs, guitar virtuosi, vocal prominence and excessively loud playing are characteristics of the style with performers having a 'macho' image of leather, motorbikes and aggression. Major bands include AC/DC, Black Sabbath, Iron Maiden and ZZ Top. *Thrash Metal* is much heavier and faster hard rock performed by groups such as Anthrax.

hillbilly

Country-style music originating in Tennessee, Kentucky and West Virginia, USA. See **country music**.

hocket (Fr., *hoquet* 'hiccup')

The practice of inserting rests for expressive purposes in vocal parts in medieval church music. Sometimes even inserted in the middle of words, but mainly in two parts, i.e. one sings whilst the other is silent. Also used in instrumental music.

homophony (Gk., 'same sounding')
Describes music where parts move together, but where the main part is a top melody accompanied by chords beneath. The opposite of **polyphonic** music where all parts are more or less equal and contrapuntal.

hondo (Sp.)
A term used in the phrase 'cante hondo' (literally 'deep song'). A sad Andalusian song involving a great deal of note repetition, melodic decoration and the use of intervals smaller than a semi-tone. Phrygian **cadence** is also a characteristic of this style.

honky tonk
'Honky' is a term used by blacks to describe whites and honky tonk is white country music as performed by singers like Hank Williams. Although steeped in the blues, Williams liked the straight no-nonsense country song with a true-to-life storyline and memorable refrain, e.g. *Cold, Cold Heart*, *I'm so Lonesome I could Cry* and *There'll be no Teardrops Tonight*. Williams also injected the more personal 'I' into songs and the honky tonk image became the man with no money, no luck, no woman and with the bar room and booze as his only friends. To God-fearing, Bible-thumping country stars like Roy Acuff and Hank Snow this music was outrageous. Other honky tonk performers included Ernest Tubb, Kitty Wells and Lefty Frizzell who sang songs like *Wild Side of Life*, *There Stands the Glass*, and *Walkin' the Floor Over You*, all about cheating, drinking and loneliness.

hornpipe
In the 16th-century the hornpipe was a lively English dance in triple time. In the 18th-century it changed to two or four beats in the bar and became associated with sailors, e.g. the sailor's hornpipe in Gilbert and Sullivan's *Ruddigore*.

humoresque (Fr.), **humoreske** (Ger.)
A term applied by composers such as Schumann and Dvorák to a capricious piece of music.

I

idée fixe (Fr., 'fixed idea')

A device of Berlioz, commonly called *motto theme*, which is a recurring theme common to all movements of a piece, but treated differently according to the demands of the dramatic scheme. The most famous example of this device is his *Symphonie Fantastique*.

idyll

a literary term (prose or verse) describing rural life and thus applied to music, e.g. Wagner's *Siegfried Idyll* (1870).

imitation

A contrapuntal method of part writing where one or more voice(s) repeats, or recognisably repeats, a motif or theme previously stated by another voice. In the 16th century this device flourished in the church and thus became a basis of the **canzona** and **ricercar**. The **canon** and **fugue** also employ imitation according to set rules.

impressionism

This term is borrowed from painting (describing the works of Monet and Degas, etc) and applied to the music of composers such as Debussy, Ravel and Delius. Impressionist music is concerned with tones and textures producing a vague feeling. However, there is always an underlying formal structure. Originating with Debussy (1862-1918), the style might better be called *symbolist*, since Debussy was influenced by the French school of symbolist poets such as Mallarmé and Verlaine. Central to this style of composition was Debussy's conception of the whole tone scale, producing a dreamy feeling. Parallel fifths, ninths, thirds, and fourths also add to this vague atmosphere. An example of this style is Debussy's *Prélude à l'après-midi d'un faune* (1892), evoking the imagery of Mallarmé's poem.

improvisation or **extemporisation**
The art of composing or inventing spontaneously, sometimes upon a given theme. Different forms occur throughout musical history, but chiefly it appears in a **cadenza** or in chorale preludes. In 20th-century popular music improvisation is a central characteristic in jazz and blues styles, where it may appear instrumentally or vocally. (See also **scat singing**.) In the 1940s **bebop** concentrated entirely upon improvisation in evolving not only melody but also harmony. In the 1960s the trumpeter Miles Davis based improvisation on modes rather than harmonies, and this led to even greater freedom for creativity. Ornette Coleman's school even eschewed the regular pulse.

incidental music
Originally, this described music for performance during the action of plays, or between scenes of plays, etc. This dated back to the Greeks, Romans and medieval times as well as being particularly important in Shakespearian and other Elizabethan plays. However, the term now includes **overtures** and **interludes**.

industrial rock
A minor musical movement of the late 1960s returning to a futuristic sound based on **noise rock** recreating the Industrial Revolution by using pipes, chains and pieces of metal found in the street. Test Departments (a British group) staged big events accompanied by machine sounds, and a German group called Collapsing New Buildings, have performed with cement mixers and jackhammers.

interlude
Generally, this term is applied to a piece of incidental music for performance during a play. However, it is also applied to instrumental music inserted between lines or verses of a song, hymn or chorale. The term can also be used as a title for an entire composition.

intermezzo (It.), **intermède** (Fr.), **intermedium** (Lat.)
This term literally means 'something in the middle', and, therefore, usually describes an instrumental piece performed between acts of plays, operas, etc. The term is also applied to a short concert piece.

invention

The term was used by J.S. Bach to describe pieces in two-part counterpoint for clavier. However, Bach's previously named *Sinfonie* for three-part pieces are now also called inventions, and the term has been used by later composers.

J

jabo (Sp.)
A slow solo dance in 3/4 time.

jacara (Sp.)
An old Spanish song dance.

jazz
Mainly originating in New Orleans at the turn of the century, with roots in black folk work songs, spirituals, **blues** and **ragtime**, jazz is a style characterised by improvisation, unique instrumental tone, **riffs**, breaks, polyrhythms and other effects. Traditional jazz was often based on the form and harmony of march tunes, greatly improvised and incorporating the flattened notes of the blues with a driving beat. Louis Armstrong went north with a unique solo style (as opposed to collective band playing in New Orleans), improvising on harmonic sequences rather than just melodies. At this point, simple instrumentation of traditional jazz bands included: (1) the rhythm section consisting of a string bass (replaced in the early days by a tuba, guitar or banjo); (2) the brass section, which played the melody or melody and harmony and was made up of cornets, trumpets and trombones; and finally, (3) two reed instruments which were initially clarinets, but were later replaced by saxophones, in the 1920s. As the style spread, the bands increased in size. In the 1930s **swing** developed, with big names like Benny Goodman and Duke Ellington. In the 1940s **bebop, bop** or **rebop** reacted against the big-band sound of swing with exponents such as Dizzy Gillespie, Art Tatum and Miles Davis. In the 1950s *cool jazz* (more light and lyrical than bebop) and *hard bop* vied for popularity. In 1960 Miles Davis began improvising on modes rather than harmonies, leading to greater freedom of structure. He also incorporated the rock music electronic sounds to provide a new jazz. In the late 1960s, Ornette Coleman developed a

compositional theory of the equal importance of harmonies, tempos and melodies, and he became a central figure in jazz avant-garde, with its all out free playing and intensity of emotion. All styles are still popular today.

jig
See **gigue**.

jodel (Ger.), **yodel** (Eng.)
A style of singing for men, common in Switzerland and the Austrian Tyrol. It involves the alternation between natural voice and falsetto. This style of singing is used for simple dance-like tunes and the effect is always cheerful.

jota
A moderately fast dance of Aragon in Northern Spain in 3/4 time accompanied by castanets and danced by couples who also sing in four-line stanzas. The jota style has been used by other composers, e.g. Glinka, Liszt and Saint-Saëns.

K

krakowiak (Pol.), **cracovienne** (Fr.)

A lively and syncopated dance from the Krakow region in Poland. It is usually danced by a large party with much heel striking and extemporised stanzas are often sung. Occasionally, only one couple will dance with dramatic actions.

L

lai or **lay**

A French song form of the 14th century consisting of twelve unequal stanzas sung to different tunes. It is similar to the **sequence**. A single stanza could also comprise one or more sections.

lament

Traditional music of elegiac character. In Scottish and Irish folk music the lament is often played on the bagpipes.

ländler

A popular Austrian dance in 3/4 time similar to the waltz, but slower. Ländler were written by some classical composers, e.g. Mozart and Beethoven.

lauda (It.)

A popular devotional song for several voices set to Italian poems and sung by the *Laudisti*, a religious confraternity, between the 14th and 18th centuries. Laudi provided an introduction to **oratorio** form.

leading motif
See **leitmotif** below.

leitmotif (Ger., 'leading-motif')
This is a recurring theme symbolising an object, character or emotion, etc., first used by H. Von Wolzogen in discussion of Wagner's *The Ring*. This device was used to strengthen the dramatic significance in a work by recalling at will the audience's memory of thoughts and actions, thus heightening emotion in the vocal line as well as in the orchestral commentary. Mozart had previously used this idea in *Don Giovanni*, and Berlioz also in his orchestral music. However, see **idée fixe**. Schumann and Liszt called it a 'metamorphosis of themes'. Other composers also adopted this principle, notably Richard Strauss.

lied (Ger., plural **lieder**)
Meaning song or songs, this term is now especially applied to the German romantic songs of Schubert, Brahms, Schumann, Wolf, etc., in which attention is paid to the mood and expression of words and the importance of the piano part.

linear counterpoint
Counterpoint in which the emphasis is on the individual value of the lines, rather than the harmonic implication. In the 20th century the term is sometimes used to describe contrapuntal writing (e.g., Stravinsky).

loure
This term has two connected meanings: (1) A type of Normandy bagpipe and (2) a rustic dance accompanied by the bagpipe rather like a **gigue**, but lower in tempo. A characteristic rhythm of this style is an accented short note followed by a long note. The loure was also adopted into ballet and orchestral music.

lullaby
see **berceuse**.

lydian mode
A set of notes (named after ancient peoples in Greek music) equivalent to the white notes on the piano from C to C. From the Middle Ages, this mode represented the white notes on

the piano from F to F, often with a flattened B, making it identical to the modern F major scale. The lydian mode was one of the four ambrosian modes. Pope Gregory later called these authentic modes. See **ambrosian chant modes**.

lyric drama
A synonym for opera, i.e. the whole class of opera, as opposed to the spoken play.

lyric opera
A rather vague term indicating an opera in which singing is more important than the drama.

lyric piece
A literary term describing a short piece, expressing feeling, e.g. the *Lyric Pieces* of Grieg and the *Lyric Suite* of Berg.

M

madrigal

A secular unaccompanied vocal composition set to poems for several parts. The madrigal originated in 14th-century Italy and was in two or three parts with a strict form. Composers at this time included Landini. By the 16th century the form became freer and similar to the **frottola**. Later, the 16th-century 'classical' madrigal was mainly written in imitative **polyphony** in five parts with word-painting. Composers at that time included Gabrieli. Palestrina and Lassus. The late madrigal style, as composed by Monteverdi or Marenzio, was more chromatic, dramatic and generally less restrained than before, and madrigals for solo, duet or trio accompanied by continuo can be found in works by Monteverdi. In the late 16th century, madrigals appeared in England with composers such as Morley, Weelkes and Wilbye who developed particularly English characteristics, influenced by the native tradition of secular song exemplified in the works of Byrd and Gibbons. Musically, English madrigals have a greater feeling of organisation. Generally, however, madrigals utilised the modal system rather than the modern keys, and this, combined with the rhythmic freedom and independent part-writing, gave the form its distinctive and rather quaint sound. See also **ballett** and **ayre**.

malagueña (Sp.)

An Andalusian folk dance from Malaga, similar to the **fandango** with improvised singing. Also an instrumental piece. A characteristic of the style is the cadence; the mode, at this point is minor and the bass of the last four chords is the descending upper part of the scale (thus arriving on the dominant) with a flattened leading note, while above this bass scale the parts move in parallel thirds, fifths and octaves. The poetry sung in the malagueña style is similar to the **jota**.

manchega (Sp.)
A bright and lively dance from La Mancha and a type of **seguidilla**.

march
A piece for marching. The times may vary, e.g. 2/4 or 6/8 for a quick march, procession or parade, and 4/4 for a slower pace, e.g. for a funeral. The main section of a march alternates in form with one or more trios.

masque, mask or **maske**
This is chiefly an elaborate 17th-century English entertainment involving poetry, dancing, scenery, instrumental and vocal music all clearly related to opera and ballet. Writers included Jonson, Beaumont and Shirley and composers included Campion and Laniere. Inigo Jones designed the scenery and machinery for some of Jonson's masques which became closer to opera with the use of **recitative**, as opposed to spoken dialogue.

mass
The principal service of the Roman Catholic Church, taken in any one of three forms: (1) high mass (*missa solemnis*), consisting of five passages of **plainsong** (*proper of the mass*) performed by a choir, deacon, sub-deacon and other ministers. These passages varied from season to season and even from day to day. The mass also consisted of five other extended passages from the congregation's part (*ordinary of the mass*), which were invariable; (2) sung mass (*missa cantata*) which is as above without the deacon or sub-deacon and (3) low mass (*missa privata* or *missa lecta*) which is usually performed by a priest and clerk. However, it is the invariable congregational *ordinary of the mass* from the high mass which constitutes what musicians mean by mass. These five 'ordinary' sections consist of the *kyrie, gloria, credo, sanctus with benedictus* and *agnus dei*. The setting of the *ordinary* as an entire musical composition developed about 1430 when unity was achieved usually by an existing plainsong melody (*cantus firmus*) and a common opening of each movement. In the 16th century, settings of the *ordinary* were in imitative **polyphony**, and from the 15th to 17th centuries settings were often performed in plainsong alternating with the organ. In the 17th century the *ordinary* was elaborated by the introduction of instrumental accompaniment with vocal combinations and also bigger settings. An example of the final stage of this tradition is Bach's B minor mass. Other

composers, e.g. Mozart, Haydn, Schubert and Beethoven also wrote settings where the overall musical conception is of prime importance.

mattinata (It., 'morning song')
Same as **alborada**.

maxixe
Originally, this was a Brazilian dance with two beats per bar of a rather strenuous nature. In the early 19th century, the dance became popular in Europe and reappeared in the early 20th century as the **tango**. However, both dances are still popular in the ballroom.

mazurka
A Polish dance in 3/4 or 3/8 time originally danced and sung. Characteristics of the style are the accentuation of the second beat of the bar, ending phrases on that beat, and dotted notes. It is a round dance with some improvisation. Chopin brought the style into concert music and wrote about 50 mazurkas, refining the dance greatly.

melisma (Gk., 'song')
A group or passage of notes sung to only one syllable. It is used in **plainsong** and is a feature of 18th-century vocal music. More generally, it describes any florid vocal passage.

melodrama
The current English meaning is a play of sensational or violent nature. However, in music history, this term is applied to spoken words with a musical background, either throughout an entire work or forming part of a work, e.g. in Beethoven's *Fidelio*.

mensural music (Lat., *musica mensurata*)
A medieval term for music with definite note-values as opposed to **plainsong** (*musica plana*).

menuet (Fr.)
See **minuet**.

Mersey beat
Beat music of the period 1963-65, influenced by The Beatles and centred around the Liverpool area. Most bands with commercial

potential signed to Brian Epstein, e.g. Gerry and the Pacemakers and The Fourmost. Other bands included The Swinging Blue Jeans and The Searchers. The characteristic of beat music is the live club feel with the influence of American rock n' roll and R&B via skiffle.

metamorphosis of themes
See **leitmotif**.

minimalism
In 1960s rock music this was a concept of music using few notes and repeating them over and over or holding notes for long periods like a drone. This corresponded with the minimalist aesthetic favouring the more detached, logical approach to Art (painting and sculpture) popular in New York. A musical exponent was LaMonte Young and artists included the sculptor, Walter De Maria. The Velvet Underground (formed in 1965), promoted this style and it eventually became the prototype of **punk** and **noise rock**.

minuet (Eng.), **menuet** (Fr.), **menuetto** (Ger.), **minuetto** (It.)
A moderately fast French dance in 3/4 time. It appeared in court circles about 1650, introduced by composers like Lully who refined it considerably. The style became most fashionable in the 18th century, later becoming one of the regular movements in the classical sonatas, symphony, string quartets, etc. of Haydn, Mozart and others, always in ternary form (minuet—trio—minuet). With Beethoven, the minuet developed into the **scherzo**.

mirror canon or **mirror fugue**
Any composition using retrograde motion or contrary motion i.e. as if a mirror were between the notes, so that one line appears to be a reflection of the other.

modes
Sets of eight-note scales inherited from ancient Greece via the Middle Ages in which they were most prevalent. However, the modes still survive in **plainsong** and much folk music. The modes may be represented by scales of white notes on the piano, with names derived from the Greek system:

I	Dorian, D-D, dominant A, final D
II	Hypodorian, A-A, dominant F, final D
III	Phrygian, E-E, dominant C, final E
IV	Hypophrygian, B-B, dominant A, final E
V	Lydian, F-F, dominant C, final F
VI	Hypolydian, C-C, dominant A, final F
VII	Mixolydian, G-G, dominant D, final G
VIII	Hypomixolydian, D-D, dominant C, final G

The following were added in the 16th century by Glareanus:

IX	Aeolian, A-A, dominant E, final A
X	Hypoaeolian, E-E, dominant C, final A
XI	Ionian, C-C, dominant G, final C
XII	Hypoionian, G-G, dominant E, final C

The 'final' of a mode is the note of a cadence or resting point in a melody, and the dominant is a 'reciting' note. Modes prefixed 'Hypo' are plagal (see **gregorian modes**) and others are 'authentic' (see **ambrosian modes** and **System of Glareanus**). Until the end of the 16th century this medieval system of modes and intervals provided bases for **polyphonic** writing. At the end of the 17th century modes had been reduced to two, now known as major and minor scales, although the major scale had been used in medieval plainsong and secular song in the form of F mode with a flattened B. In the 19th century modal idioms were of some importance in the style of impressionist composers such as Debussy and Ravel.

moment musical

An early 19th-century term used in titles of short romantic piano pieces, e.g. by Schubert.

monody (Gk., 'single song')

A solo song with accompaniment usually describing a 17th-century style of Italian solo voice and **continuo**, which exploited the expressive qualities of a performer, e.g. in opera. However, solo songs with lute were also common in the 16th century. This style was in direct contrast to earlier polyphonic writing in which all parts were equal.

monophony (Gk., 'single sound')

This term describes music consisting of one line only, unsupported by harmony or other independent melodies. Occasionally, the term is used to describe an independent melody with a simple accompaniment.

monothematic
Compositions involving the development of only one simple theme.

motet
A form, flourishing in the 13th century, which was a short piece of unaccompanied sacred music in two, three or four parts based on an existing **plainsong** melody, sung by a tenor. Other parts often had different music and words which may have been sacred or secular. Between 1300 and 1450, composers such as Machaut and Dunstable perfected a type of work known as the *isorhythmic motet*, which was usually in three parts woven around the tenor, each with the same rhythm being applied to successive divisions or repetitions of melody. At this time, motets might be written for special occasions, and they could be either sacred or secular. From 1450 to 1600, the form was mainly sacred, unaccompanied and based on a Latin text, with each part having the same words. The plainsong tenor basis was still used but a more imitative style with new themes was more common. Later motets (now always sacred) were set in styles of the period, some with instrumental accompaniment and some with choir and voices.

motif (Fr.)
Occasionally, this term implies **leitmotif**.

motiv (Ger.), **motive** (Eng.)
A short and brief independent melody or rhythmic unit which may be as short as two notes, or longer, and is repeated. See also **leitmotif**.

motown
A record company formed in Detroit, Michigan by black business man, Berry Gordy Jr. in 1960, with a string of labels, including *Tamla*, which amalgamated into the Motown corporation. Gordy began with R&B sounds aimed at a white market, and later signed Smokey Robinson, Lamont Dozier and Eddie Holland to write and produce their own records and others. The Supremes, The Four Tops and Stevie Wonder were also signed. A characteristic of the motown sound was the gospel element, initially via Aretha Franklin, daughter of the Rev. C.L. Franklin. The call and response patterns and accompaniments used in gospel were injected into the solid R&B beat. Early songs like *Dancing in the Street* by Martha and the Vandellas (later

popular for Bowie and Jagger in the 80s) and *Baby Love* by The Supremes, both of 1964, were examples. The combination of R&B and gospel soon became known as **soul** music. Other motown soul stars were Diana Ross, Marvin Gaye, Lionel Richie and Rick James.

motto or **motto theme**
A recurring theme with symbolic significance. This device is related to **leitmotif** and also to **idée fixe**.

mouth music, **port a beul** (Gael.)
Wordless but articulated singing accompanying Scottish Highland dancing. Known in Ireland as 'lilting' and in the Scottish lowlands as 'diddling'. This occurs where no instruments are available.

movement
A self-contained section of music of a large composition, e.g. a sonata or symphony, usually having a separate indication of speed. However, it is possible for a movement to be connected to others and therefore, it need not be considered as wholly independent.

musette (Fr.)
A type of French bagpipe, popular in Louis XIV's time, with the title also being given to a type of **gavotte** using a drone bass, suggestive of the bagpipe.

musica da camera (It.)
See **chamber music**.

musica figurata (It.)
This term has two meanings: (1) polyphonic music in which the parts have rhythmic and melodic independence as opposed to note against note writing and (2) (a less common meaning) **plainsong** with a decorated melody, also known as *musica colorata*.

musica reservata (Lat.)
A late 16th-century term to describe the giving of vivid expression to words, and also music, for private occasions.

musical
This term is an abbreviation of 'musical play'. The musical

originated as musical comedy which was closely related to **operetta**. Mainly American-influenced, the musical started as light stage entertainment, often transforming into films. The first Hollywood film musical starring Al Jolson was *The Jazz Singer* (1927), originally a stage-musical. Other early film musicals included *Top Hat* with Fred Astaire and Ginger Rogers, *Gold Diggers* and *Meet Me in St Louis* with Judy Garland. The 1950s produced *Singin' In The Rain*, *Gentlemen Prefer Blondes* and *Seven Brides For Seven Brothers*. The 1960s injected more realism into the musical with films like *Sweet Charity* including the famous song *Hey, Big Spender* and musical films of the 1970s include *On A Clear Day You Can See Forever*. Early songwriters for musical films were George and Ira Gershwin (*Lady Be Good*), Rodgers and Hart (*Blue Moon, Pal Joey*) and Rodgers and Hammerstein II (*Oklahoma, Carousel, South Pacific, The Sound of Music*). In the UK Andrew Lloyd Webber and Tim Rice wrote the stage-musicals *Joseph and the Amazing Technicolour Dreamcoat* (1968), *Jesus Christ Superstar* (1970) and *Evita* (1976). The 1980s stage-musical *Starlight Express*, written by Andrew Lloyd Webber and Richard Stilgoe introduced highly technical stage effects to the musical.

musical switch
A collection or medley of well-known tunes, of which only snippets are played before being 'switched' on to the next melody.

music drama
A Wagnerian term to describe his new concept of opera based on leitmotifs and fusing scenery, costume, libretti, music and drama into a new art for which the term, **opera**, was inadequate.

musique concrète (Fr.) or **concrete music**
This style describes the collaging of real sounds, pre-recorded on tape. In the 1940s Peter Schaeffer coined the phrase. He and his Paris associates believed music of the past to be 'abstract' (i.e. written symbols were used as a starter) and that therefore music of the future, incorporating new technology with pre-recorded real or instrumental sounds as starters, must be 'concrete'. With composer Pierre Henri in the 1950s Schaeffer created a symphony, an opera and also a studio which was greatly used by Pierre Boulez. At first the term was used in contrast to electronic music which was created purely with synthetic sounds. However,

Varèse and Stockhausen combined these two techniques and since then the term has become somewhat old fashioned.

muzak

The general meaning of this term is 'canned' background music, heard in such places as lifts, restaurants, airports and hotels and to be listened to or totally ignored. It was also the basis, however, of many developments in 20th-century music, e.g. **furniture music** or **ambient music**.

N

nachtanz (Ger., 'following dance')

A quick dance, usually in triple time, to contrast with a previous slow dance in duple time. The term is applied to dances in pairs, dating from the 15th—17th centuries, e.g. *Pavane and Galliard, Allemande and Courante* or *Sarabande and Gigue*.

nachtmusik (Ger., 'night music')

This term describes music with a serenade-like character,and is often applied to a suite, e.g. Mozart's *Eine Kleine Nachtmusik, K. 525.*

nachtstück (Ger., 'night piece')

A term with two meanings: (1) the equivalent of **nocturne** and (2) a piece of music of solemn character.

Napolitana

A simple and light style of madrigal of possibly Neapolitan origin similar to the **villanella**. In the 20th century, the term is applied to a type of music hall song in which a characteristic is to have verses in the minor and choruses in the major.

neo-classicism

A 20th-century trend reacting against emotional romanticism, by adopting the classical principals of balance, objectivity, economic writing, contrapuntal writing, diatonic and chromatic harmonies, smaller instrumental forces and generally structured forms with lighter texture. Neo-classicism arose as a result of a search for order in musical writing other than serialism and a vast knowledge of past styles which could be drawn upon and used in new ways. Notable composers included Stravinsky who wrote *Oedipus Rex* (1927) and *The Rake's Progress* (1951) in this style. However, Stravinsky and Hindemith were also greatly influenced by the Baroque period.

neo-romantic

A vague term describing the 20th-century reaction of some composers against **neo-classicism**. Occurred mainly in the 1920s.

new age music

A 20th-century style using eastern classical music emphasising improvisational and floating qualities at the expense of rhythm. Melodies are sweet, slow and sad, with pretty harmonies and the occasional real noise like a wave or a seagull. Instrumentations involve great use of synthesisers with 'delay' effect. Phrases are repeated, expressing a mournful feeling as they fade out. Composers include Deuter, Kitaro and Harold Budd. This meditative, 'lost-in-space' sound is similar to the 'psychedelic' 1960s scene.

new music

A term with two historical meanings: (1) In the 17th century it was the expressive music being pioneered by Caccini and others, with more word painting, contrasts and the recreation of ancient Greek music and drama; (2) In the 19th century it described the music of Liszt and Wagner which was of a more 'progressive' nature as opposed to the more traditional music of Brahms.

new romantic

A late 1970s and early 1980s new wave rock style, mainly disco-influenced with emphasis on an outrageous but sophisticated and elegant image. The video was also essential, especially to new romantic star Adam Ant who was tutored by punk instigator, Malcolm Maclaren. Maclaren introduced Ant to a tribal drum with chant sound, first made popular by Gary Glitter in the 1970s, but manipulated by Ant to appeal to the adolescent. Ant modelled himself on images of Prince Charming, the red indian and the pirate and crashed his way through the charts with *Stand and Deliver* (1981) and *Goody Two Shoes* (1982). Other new romantic performers included Spandau Ballet, Duran Duran and Human League.

new wave

Progressive **punk rock**.

nocturne

Generally a night-piece, first introduced by John Field and

perfected by Chopin. It is characteristically a slow piano piece with a lyrical graceful melody, which is later greatly embellished. This style belongs to the romantic period of music.

noise music

This is 20th-century music evoking the everyday outside world by using non-musical instruments (i.e. not accepted orchestral music) or combining instruments in such a way as to make new sounds. Rossolo believed 'noise' began in the 19th century at the advent of the industrial revolution. However, it was not until 1920 that noise was accepted with the work of Varèse. In 1923 *Hyperprism* combined conventional wind instruments with percussion to produce discords. *Ionisation* (1933), which was scored for 33 percussion instruments, a piano (playing tone clusters) and some specially designed wood and metal objects, created an unheard-of wide variety of timbre. Police whistles and car horns reflected the everyday street sounds, but they were written in with character and meaning so that noise was acceptable as music. After World War II John Cage with his **prepared piano** style influenced composers in both America and Europe. Partch (an American), built his own instruments with glass bottles etc., and even devised a special tuning system. Berio, Stockhausen and Penderecki, although not inventing their own instruments, produced new and odd sounds. Early concerts were serious affairs, often having a mystical or ritualistic air, with musicians dressed in party masks playing percussion. These sonic illustrations were therefore part of an interplay of harmonies and counterpoints. See also **minimalism** and **industrial rock**.

noise rock, art rock, rock concrete

A vague term describing a style similar to **punk** and **minimalism**.

note-row

See **serial music**.

O

one-step

Originally an American ballroom dance, popular world-wide in the early 20th century. The one-step is more energetic than the fox-trot and has two beats per bar.

open harmony

A style of harmony in which chords are spread widely, as opposed to close harmony.

opera (It. and Sp.), **opéra** (Fr.), **oper** (Ger.)

Generally, this is a dramatic work in which most characters sing with an instrumental accompaniment. Historically, precursors are found in associations between music and drama, e.g. in the liturgical dramas of the Middle Ages and in the 16th-century Italian court entertainments. However, present-day opera dates from the Florentine *Camerata*, a group of musicians, artists and scholars, led by Count Bardi. Members of the *Camerata* were opposed to vocal polyphonic music because they believed that it destroyed poetry. They also believed that, when set to music, words should be recited without too much interpretation. This concept became known as **recitative**. Monteverdi's *Orfeo* (1607) is an important example of the Florentine philosophy, but musically goes far beyond earlier forms by employing a lavish orchestra, the use of recitative with contrasting strophic songs, choral writing and a great intensity of emotions. This opera was amongst the first to use arias and duets, thus relieving the monotony of recitative. In the 17th century opera spread throughout Europe. With *Cadmus at Hermione* (1673), Lully introduced the form into France, a country incorporating ballet until the 19th century. Purcell's *Dido and Aeneas* was England's first true opera, greatly influenced by the **masque**. Scarlatti and Stradello developed the Italian traditions out of which emerged a standard type of **aria** in *da capo* form and overtures in three movements. However, in the 18th century the rigidity of opera was a cause for concern; dramatic and musical expression, for example, became subservient to vocal virtuosity. Gluck and Rameau reacted against this and developed a simpler style, and many types of opera began to appear in the 18th century, e.g. **opera buffa, opera seria** and **opéra comique**. In the 19th century **grand opera** developed in Paris. In Germany Wagner, who was influenced by both grand opera and the romantic movement believed that opera should combine all the arts. He called his operas **music dramas**. However, some composers retained the Italian style, e.g. Bellini and Donizetti, while Rossini, who gave the orchestra greater importance, also broke recitative and solo vocal improvisation conventions. Verdi developed this new approach in *Otello* (1887) showing considerable dramatic and orchestral control. In Russia and Czechoslovakia, nationalism appeared in the works of Glinka, Mussorgsky, Borodin and Rimsky-Korsakov. In the 20th century, opera is diverse. In Germany, Wagner initially influenced operas like Richard Strauss's *Der Rosen Kavalier.* In France, impressionism was strong. *Verismo* (realism) was forceful in Italy, e.g. in Puccini's *Madame Butterfly*. Britten, Stravinsky and Berg are also prominent 20th-century opera composers.

opéra-ballet (Fr.)
A stage work flourishing in France in the 17th and 18th centuries. Song and dance were of equal importance and chief exponents included Lully and Rameau.

opéra-bouffe (Fr.)
A type of French comic opera. The term was derived from **opera buffa** (It.), but with a slightly different definition. This term describes light but satirical operas or operettas, e.g. those of Offenbach.

opera buffa (It.)
Chiefly an 18th-century Italian comic opera, different from **opera seria** in that it chose lighter subjects and music with everyday characters, e.g. Pergolesi's *The Maid as Mistress* and Mozart's *The Marriage of Figaro*.

opéra-comique (Fr., 'comic opera')
There are two historical meanings: (1) in the 18th century this was a type of French comic opera with spoken dialogue usually of

a lighter style than serious operas and (2) in the 19th century this term was applied to any opera (serious or comic) with spoken dialogue, e.g. Bizet's *Carmen*.

opera seria (It., 'serious opera')
The term is chiefly applied to the 17th- and early 18th-century operas characterised by an Italian libretto involving an heroic or mythological plot with a general air of formality. Leading roles were often given to castrato singers. This style is the opposite of **opera buffa**.

operetta (It., 'little opera')
Virtually synonymous with light opera. The term is mainly used to describe the 19th-century type of opera with dialogue. Characteristic elements of the style are tunes of a popular nature telling of romance and comedy and poking fun at serious opera. Offenbach, Johann Strauss and Sullivan are among the chief exponents of this genre.

oratorio
A musical composition consisting of a setting of a sacred text for soloists, chorus and orchestra in dramatic form. The term originated in the late 16th century from St Philip Neri's decision to hold more attractive popular services in an oratory, hence the title 'oratorio'. Early forms demanded scenery, costumes and action. Carissimi was an early exponent who adopted opera forms, especially the use of the chorus which reflected upon the dramatic action. Later Italian composers included A. Scarlatti and Rossini and other major writers were J.S. Bach, Handel, Haydn, Mendelssohn, Elgar and Vaughan Williams.

organum (Lat.)
A medieval form of part-writing based on **plainsong**. In the 9th century the added part follows the plainsong in parallel fifths or fourths but also in thirds and in unison. In the 11th and 12th centuries octaves fifths and fourths (i.e. perfect intervals) were written above the plainsong. By the 12th century the added part was more florid in style. See also **motet**.

ostinato (It.)
A persistently repeated musical figure or rhythm. Quite often an ostinato appears in the bass and this is called a *basso ostinato* or **ground bass**.

overture

Generally, this is orchestral introductory music to an opera, oratorio, play or ballet. However, there are other meanings: (1) it may be a one-movement orchestral work composed for the concert hall, e.g. Mendelssohn's *Hebrides*, entitled with an allusion to a non-musical subject which is now called a 'concert overture'; (2) in the 17th and 18th centuries the French overture (i.e. preceding an opera, etc.) was in three movements, slow—quick—slow; the Italian overture (a precursor of the **symphony**), also in three movements, was quick—slow—quick; (3) after Wagner's *Lohengrin* (1847), operas sometimes opened with a **prelude**, often shorter than an overture and leading straight in to Act I.

P

palindrome

A word, verse or sentence which can be read backwards or forwards, e.g. the group ABBA or the word 'madam'. In music the term indicates works which repeat the music backwards at certain points. Occasionally this device can be found in the tonal music of Haydn and Mozart. In atonal music it provides a form on which to build, although repetition is never exact. An example is Berg's *Chamber Concerto*.

pandiatonicism

Experimentalist composer Nicolas Slonimsky coined the term to indicate the free use of all the notes of the diatonic scale in non-resolving chords, e.g. the added sixth and ninth popular in jazz. Most composers favour C major when writing in this style, and the sense of tonality is strong because of few chromatics. An example is Stravinsky's ballet *Pulcinella*.

pantomime

Nowadays this is a popular Christmas show acting out a fairy-tale or traditional story involving speech and popular music. Originally the form began in ancient Greece with music but no words. In the 18th century characters such as the harlequin and clown were taken from the Italian *commedia dell'arte*, which in turn developed into the modern form with songs, influenced by André Warser's *L'Enfant Prodigue* written in 1890. Pantomimes today include *Cinderella, Puss in Boots* and *Aladdin*.

pantonality

Schönberg's preferred term for **atonality**.

parody mass (Lat., *missa parodia)*

A polyphonic mass using existing music from motets or chansons and written in more or less complete sections. This term has only been used since the 19th century, but the device had been adopted by earlier composers such as Palestrina (1524-94).

partita (It.), **partie** (Fr.), **parthie** (Ger.)
Commonly this term describes a **suite,** but it can also describe an air with variations.

part song
Popular in Britain, this is generally a strophic song for several male, female or mixed voices in which there are many singers to a part. Usually the top part has the principal melody. Many composers wrote part songs including Elgar, Parry and Stanford.

paso doble (Sp., 'double step')
A 1920s popular dance in 2/4 or 6/8 time.

passacaglia (It.), **passecaille** (Fr.)
A 17th-century slow and stately dance in triple time with regular phrases of two, four or eight bars each ending with a perfect cadence. The style first appeared in keyboard music and later simply became a piece in which a theme is continually repeated. French composers wrote their passacaglias in **rondo form** while German composers wrote in variation form over a ground bass. This style is similar to the **chaconne**.

passage work
A section of music often of no great thematic interest and used for virtuoso display.

passa mezzo (It.)
Popular in England, Germany and France in the late 16th century, this is a dance in duple time. Originally, the melody was sung by the dancers and was followed by a **salterello** in triple time.

passepied (Fr.)
Popular in Brittany, this is a quick dance in triple time. In the mid-17th century the passepied was introduced into French ballet and it became an optional item of the suite. Lully and other French composers used it in their operas. In England it is called *paspy*.

passion music
This is the Passion of Christ, as accounted by Matthew, Mark, Luke and John, set to music and performed during Holy Week. In the Middle Ages settings were in **plainsong** with contrasts in vocal ranges and speed to donote the characters. In the 15th century polyphonic singing was introduced for the *turba* (crowds) and certain individual characters. In the 16th century the settings of whole texts in polyphony began with occasional use of plainsong as a *cantus firmus* in the tenor. Schütz, Byrd and Lassus were composers who wrote in this style. Lutheran composers introduced new operatic features after 1640, including recitative, arias and the dramatic use of instruments. Chorales were also introduced, leading to a development of the oratorio style of passion around 1700. Famous works include Bach's *St John* (1723) and *St Matthew* (1729) Passions.

pasticcio (It., 'pie')
Common in 18th-century operas, this is a device of selecting and compiling pieces of music from various composers to form an entire work.

pastorale (It.)
This term describes stage entertainment based around a rustic or legendary theme originally with little or no music. However, during the 18th century the style became more operatic, e.g. Handel's opera *Acis and Galatea*. It also describes an instrumental movement similar to the **musette** with long drone-like bass notes in 6/8 or 12/8 time.

patter song
Popular in opera, this is a comic song in which words are sung as fast as possible. The words are often tongue-twisters and the style is often found in the operettas of Gilbert and Sullivan.

pavane or **pavan, pavana, paven, pavin**
A slow court dance in duple time employing repetitive steps, from Italy. The style was introduced in the early 16th century and was developed especially by the English virginalists who followed it with a **galliard** often using the same theme.

pedal point
Generally known as 'pedal' and common in sonata form, this is usually a bass note held while harmonic progressions continue

above. The two may or may not be concordant. A pedal on the tonic usually comes at the end of a piece. Folk music drones are also a form of pedal point.

pentatonic
A five-note scale, the commonest being without minor seconds, e.g. CDEGAC. A pentatonic scale can also be played by simply striking the black notes on the piano. The pentatonic scale forms the basis of Scottish and Irish folk songs, e.g. *Auld Lang Syne* and much traditional Chinese, Japanese and Far Eastern music.

perpetual canon
Popularly known as a **round**, this is a whole canon repeating itself. It is also known as an *infinite canon*.

perpetuum mobile (Lat., 'perpetually in motion')
A fast piece of music in which there is a rapid repetitive note-pattern played throughout. Paganini's *Moto Perpetuo*, op. 11 is an example.

phase music
Originated by Steve Reich in the 1960s, this is music of great intensity obtained by taping short rhythmic modules which are repeated and overlapped by using tape loops. Early examples include *Come Out* and *Melodica* (1966) and *Drumming* (1971). In *The Desert Music* (1984), Reich uses canons and, although abandoning purely electronic music with the use of standard orchestral players the canons themselves have a phase effect.

pibroch (Gael., *piobaireachd* 'pipe-tune')
A form of Scottish bagpipe music, consisting of variations on a theme called *urlar*, involving grace notes and the *leumluath, taorluath* and *crunluath* movements. A famous example is the tune *Cha Till Mac Cruimein* (Mac Crimmon Will Never Return).

plainsong or **plainchant** (Lat., *cantus planus*)
This term is applied generally to the unaccompanied melody to which the Roman Catholic liturgical texts are sung. Plainsong is free in rhythm, like speech and is unmetrical. It is divided into two groups: (1) the *responsorial* which is derived from reciting psalms round the dominant and (2) the *antiphonal* which developed as melody. However, the final form of plainsong called **gregorian chant** is still used in the Roman Catholic

church today. See also **ambrosian chant** and **modes** for information on the beginnings of order in church music.

polka
A popular dance in fairly quick 2/4 time originating in 19th-century Bohemia. Smetana (1824-84), the Bohemian composer, wrote polkas, e.g. in *The Bartered Bride*.

polo
A syncopated fairly fast Andalusian folk dance in 3/4 time with characteristic ornamental phrases like *Ay*. An example of the polo is in the prelude to the fourth Act in Bizet's *Carmen*.

polonaise (Fr.), **polacca** (It.)
A moderately fast Polish dance in 3/4 time with a repeated stately rhythmic pattern. The most famous polonaises are those written by Chopin.

polska
A Scandinavian dance, originating in Poland. It is in 3/4 time and derived from the **mazurka**.

polyphony
A style of music in two or more parts in which each part is independent and of equal importance. These parts often move in different directions and at different times. Therefore, polyphonic music as it is commonly used implies counterpoint. Present in the works of Palestrina, Lassus and Byrd in the 16th and early 17th centuries and later in the works of J.S. Bach. However, in the baroque era polyphony was determined by harmony, whereas previously the polyphony itself was more important. The opposite of this term is **homophony**.

pop music
A general term for modern commercial music. The **rock 'n' roll** craze of the 1950s is generally accepted as the first pop music. The original pop song, therefore, is *Rock Around the Clock* by Bill Haley and the Comets (1955).

port a beul (Gael.)
Same as **mouth music**.

prelude, **prélude** (Fr.), **präludium** (Ger.)

Generally, this is an introductory piece of music. Each of the 48 fugues of Bach is preceded by a prelude in any regular form, but in the same key as the fugue. Preludes in the baroque suite were of a free nature similar to the virgin, organ and lute preludes of the 15th and 16th centuries. Chopin's 24 preludes were romantic in style, but like Bach's 48 involved the complete key cycle with a single theme. .Debussy and Rachmaninoff also wrote preludes following the same plan, but not following the complete key cycle. Wagner and others, after 1840, wrote short informal orchestral pieces as preludes to operas rather than the formal **overture**, e.g. in Wagner's *Lohengrin* and in Verdi's *La Traviata*. Wagner uses the word 'vorspiel' for his introductory pieces.

prepared piano

A 20th-century technique of inserting objects between the piano strings for performance. The style was introduced and entitled by composer, John Cage. An early example of prepared piano in Cage's work is *Second Construction* (1940) which involves a screw and a piece of cardboard. Later pieces, e.g. *Sonatas and Interludes*, have 45 preparations with strict instructions as to where the objects are to be inserted. However, these new sounds contain an element of chance since the piano and objects may not always be of exactly the same nature. The prepared piano, therefore, allows both the composer and performer more freedom to experiment and this concept changed the whole meaning of traditional notation. Although prepared piano music is notated normally, the sounds themselves are different and so a score became a means of instruction to the performer. Cage wrote a concerto for prepared piano in 1950, but has since not returned to this style of writing.

programme music or **programmatic music**

Music which interprets or describes a story, poem, painting, landscape or emotional experience. It is the opposite of **absolute music**. Berlioz' *Symphonie Fantastique* is an example but Liszt's **symphonic poems** were so accurate in depicting their subject that he provided audiences and listeners with a programme or preface in case there should be any misinterpretation. Liszt described composers of programme music as 'tone-poets' and Richard Strauss (1864-1949) introduced pictorial possibilities into orchestral writing with his tone-poems *Till Eulenspiegel's Merry Pranks* and *Don Quixote*.

protest music

Bob Dylan started this 1960s folk music style, initially using traditional folk instruments like the acoustic guitar and harmonica. He sang about controversial political topics of the day and appealed to the 1960s intellectual student generation whose hopes for peace in a world without bombs and racism had led to widespread marches and demonstrations. Protest music reflected these feelings. Joan Baez, Woody Guthrie and Pete Seeger (writer of *Where Have all the Flowers Gone*) all sang in a similar mould. Bob Dylan's protest music featured in the albums *Free Wheelin' Bob Dylan* (1963) and *The Times They are A—Changin'* (1964). However, Dylan rather distrusted the folk scene and moved into more personalised music after 1964.

psychedelic rock

This style was inspired by The Beatle's album *Sergeant Pepper's Lonely Heart's Club Band* in 1967, with its surrealism, LSD experiences and dreamlike qualities through songs like *Lucy in the Sky with Diamonds*. Otherwise known as 'acid rock', bands like The Who and The Rolling Stones soon produced psychedelic discs. In San Francisco, bands including Quicksilver Messenger Service and The Grateful Dead wrote inner acid-influenced fantasies. A major characteristic of psychedelic rock was the light show, incorporating the use of visuals as well as sound, needed to reproduce the whole LSD experience. The Electric Circus, a New York club, enticed people into a major theatre where songs could be lengthened to hours to recapture an acid trip. Performers like Jimmy Hendrix would play such ecstatic guitar that he would sometimes finish by smashing the instrument to keep the show on a high. Pete Townsend of The Who did the same. This style encouraged more theatre in rock music.

punk rock

Punk music emerged from rejections of glam rock and rock 'n' roll which left the mid-1970s teenagers with no music to call their own. In a quest to search for new sounds, the club scenes showed most energy and ideas. Malcolm Maclaren, an art student and boutique owner went to New York, principally to manage a band called The Dolls and came back to the UK crammed with ideas for a new movement. His boutique called 'Let it Rock' changed suddenly to 'Sex' and instead of selling 1950s gear sold ripped T-shirts held together with safety-pins, and bondage-wear and caused a sensation. Teenagers flocked and Maclaren discovered a group called The Swankers, and soon, with a change of line-up, they became the notorious Sex Pistols. With Johnny Rotten as their offensive and arrogant lead singer, they gate-crashed into concerts and played, gradually acquiring a cult. Punk was about the working class, no education, anarchy and sex. It was hard, noisy and fast, played around two chords with sustained dissonance. The Sex Pistols sang *Pretty Vacant, God Save the Queen* and *Anarchy in the UK*. Other groups followed: The Ruts, The Slits, The Damned, The Buzzcocks and The Vibrators. Most politically orientated were The Clash. In the New York art world punk inspired musicians to experiment with distorted rock sounds and it became variously known as noise, rock art and rock concrete.

Q

quadrille
Originally a square dance, the quadrille became fashionable in early 19th-century France, appearing in Britain in 1815 and Germany in 1821. Danced by two or four couples, this dance became established as having five alternating parts in 6/8 and 2/4 time. The quadrille form is often evident in operatic music.

quodlibet (Lat., 'what you will')
An amalgamation of two or more popular songs to form a medley. This style was especially popular in the 17th and 18th centuries with German composers. Bach used a quodlibet at the end of his *Goldberg Variations*.

R

ragtime

This style began as dance music ('ragging') in the late 19th century and was replaced by jazz in the 1920s. Mostly a piano music style, ragtime involves highly syncopated right-hand melodies contrasted with a steady but leaping left hand. Chromaticism is also a feature and pieces are played mainly in 2/2 or 4/4 time. Scott Joplin (1868-1917) was the most famous composer of ragtime music. The film, *The Sting*, popularised his music once again in the 1970s. Examples of piano ragtime pieces by Scott Joplin include *The Maple Leaf Rag* and *The Entertainer* (theme music from *The Sting*).

rapping

Originating in the Bronx, this style of music is a combination of talk-chanting and repeating phrases to the beat of the synthesiser. 'Rap' inspired breakdancing (both are performed together) and 'scratching', which is the mixing of beats of different songs on two turntables. Rapping became extremely popular in discos.

rebop

Same as **bebop**.

recitative or **récit, récitatif** (Fr.), **rezitativ, sprechgesang** (Ger.), **recitativo** (It.)

Generally this is a style of singing used in opera and oratorio for dialogue and some narrative which is more closely related to dramatic speech in pitch and rhythm than song. Originating in the late 16th century with Florentine composers such as Peri, it was introduced into operas, oratorios and cantatas during the early 17th century. At this point recitative was accompanied by a continuo instrument, e.g. harpsichord or organ with perhaps a string bass. In 18th and 19th century operas *recitative secco* or 'dry recitative' was the accepted style. This was sung quickly in a free rhythm with only an occasional broken chord from a harpsichord or 'cellos, and sometimes with the bass line reinforced by a double-bass. *Recitative stromentato* or *recitative accompagnato* was more expressive, accompanied by the orchestra and often used to modulate to an aria. With Wagner, recitative and aria became hard to distinguish since both were taken into the vocal line. See also **sprechgesang** for the 20th-century meaning.

reel

A fast dance for two or more couples standing face to face performing figures of eight. Usually the reel is in quick 4/4 or 2/4 time in four-bar phrases. It is a national dance of Scotland but is also found in Ireland and Scandinavia.

reggae

With roots in African and traditional Caribbean music, reggae was transformed by New Orleans R&B styles. Early characteristics are emphasis on the off-beat (influenced by Fats Domino and 1940s and 1950s R&B jump bands), and lots of brass. This new beat became known as **ska** and in Britain *bluebeat*. Original performers include Byron Lee and Prince Buster. In the mid-60s ska became reggae with the brass emphasis shifting to bass and rhythm guitars and lyrics becoming more socially aware. This electric sound made reggae more accessible to white audiences and in 1966 Bob Marley and the Wailers produced *Rude Boy*. Reggae started to appear in the charts, e.g. Desmond Decker's *Israelites* (a number one chart hit of 1969) and Dave and Ansell Collin's *Double Barrel* (a number one hit in 1970). Johnny Nash brought commercial acceptance in America with songs penned by Marley, e.g. *Stir it Up*, and also helped introduce Marley to Britain. Rastafarianism was preached by Marley who provided Eric Clapton with the number one hit *I Shot the Sheriff* in 1973. In 1975 Marley's own album *Natty Dread* became a hit with the eternal *No Woman No Cry*.

requiem

The Roman Catholic mass for the dead sung to plainsong and beginning with the words 'Requiem aeternam dona eis, Domine'. The requiem may also be a choral work commemorating the dead with a different text, e.g. the text for Delius' *Requiem* was compiled by Nietzsche and Britten's *War Requiem* was set to poems by Wilfred Owen and Latin texts.

rhapsody

A 19th- and 20th-century title given by composers writing in one movement to music suggestive of romantic, heroic or nationalistic character, e.g. Liszt's *Hungarian Rhapsodies*.

rhythm 'n' blues

A style of black music, also known as 'city blues', which originated in the 1940s out of a harsh, loud and more aggressive country blues, using drums, electric guitars and saxophones. Chicago was the main centre and musicians like T-Bone Walker, Ray Charles, B.B. King, Muddy Waters and Bo Diddley played in this style. In the early 1960s an R&B movement developed in London influencing groups like the Rolling Stones to contrast with the neat and tidy style of The Beatles from Liverpool.

ricercar (It.)

A contrapuntal composition current in the 16th-18th centuries. This style often had strict imitation based on one or more themes and was in 4/2 time. Later types of ricercari, involving only one theme, are fugues (e.g. by Bach).

riff

In popular music, this is a reiterated phrase, often in the bass, played over changing harmonies and developed.

rigadoon (Eng.), **rigadoun** (Fr.)

A lively Provencal dance in 2/2 time. In the late 17th century it was introduced into the suite and ballet of French operas.

rispetto (It.)

An improvised Italian folk-poem sung to popular tunes.

rockabilly

With a flavour of country music (from hillbilly), rockabilly was the original southern rock 'n' roll. It was much less sophisticated (with its **blue grass** influences) than the northern rock n' roll groups like Bill Haley and the Comets. Hectic, energetic rhythms, frenzied singing, jittery lead-guitar playing, bass-slapping and wild vocal noises like hiccups, shrieks and stutters were characteristics of the style. In their early days Elvis Presley and Carl Perkins performed in this style although it predominated in the southern states of Tennessee and Virginia. In the late 1970s rockabilly had a revival with groups like The Stray Cats, The

Polecats and the Blue Cats. The rockabilly look was characterised by outrageous hair quiffs, styled with large amounts of hair gel.

rock 'n' roll

A 1950s style coined by the U.S. Disc Jockey, Alan Freed, rock 'n' roll was originally black R&B music which was not initially playable on white radio stations. Freed invented the name to allow air-time on his New York radio station, and within a few months rock 'n' roll had become a teenage sensation. Bill Haley and the Comets had the first world-wide hit with *Rock Around the Clock* (1955) from the film *Blackboard Jungle* starring the teenage rebel James Dean. Youngsters with money to spend after World War II were desperate for their own culture and immersed themselves in this new movement. *Shake, Rattle and Roll*, *Rip It Up* and *See You Later Alligator* were other hits for Haley. Meanwhile, a truck driver from Tupelo, Mississippi, ten years Haley's junior, called Elvis Presley was singing black music extremely well. After his first hit *Heartbreak Hotel* (1956), Elvis developed an outrageous style, tame nowadays, but shocking in the 1950s. Moving and wiggling his hips wildly to the music, letting his hair fall down and leering and grinning at the girls were all part of his image. The Establishment was sure that Elvis was to be the downfall of young people. *Hound Dog*, *Blue Suede Shoes*, *Jailhouse Rock* and *I Got Stung* were songs in the rock 'n' roll style. Many other rock 'n' rollers like Jerry Lee Lewis with *Great Balls of Fire* (1957), Chuck Berry with *Memphis Tennessee*, *Johnny B. Good* and *Roll Over Beethoven*, Buddy Holly with *Everyday*, *Heartbreak* and *That'll Be the Day*, Little Richard with *Tutti Frutti* and *Lucille*, Eddie Cochrane with *Summertime Blues* and *C'mon Everybody* and Gene Vincent with *Be Bop a Lula*. Britain's first rock 'n' roll star was Tommy Steele with *Rock with the Cavemen* (1956), followed by *Singing the Blues*. Cliff Richard also sang in this style and had a hit with *Move It*.

rock-steady

A term derived from the song *Rock Steady* performed by the Jamaican singer Anton Ellis. The style is representative of the period in the mid to late 1960s between the **ska** and **reggae** movements. Rock-steady is a slowing-down of the ska beat, with less humour and an injection of the **motown** sound together with the samba and bossa nova rhythms. Bob Marley's early songs were in the rock-steady style.

rococo
See **style galant**.

romance, romanze (Ger.), **romanza** (It.)
Widely used to describe an intimate and lyrical piece for vocal or instrumental music. Examples include Mendelssohn's *Songs Without Words* which in French are called *Romances Sans Paroles* and Mozart's slow middle movement in the piano concerto in D minor, K466 (1785) which is entitled *Romanze*.

romanesca
An harmonic bass line pattern used for variations during the mid-16th to early 17th centuries.

romantic music
A 19th-century style, romanticism was expressed through writers such as Victor Hugo and George Sand, painters such as Turner and Constable and musicians such as Paganini, Berlioz, Liszt, Rossini and Chopin. Romanticism found a new freedom of expression: there was an upsurge in nationalism and patriotism, a love of the distant past and exotic subjects and a unifying of all the arts. Great emphasis on the virtuoso performer and composer meant that society regarded the artist as a rather remote genius. Yet at the same time, the use of folk idioms brought the musician closer to the people. Emotional aspects now governed traditional formal musical structures, but in order to achieve unity, **cyclic form** and the concepts of recurring ideas such as **motto theme**, **idée fixe** and **leitmotif** were introduced. Other forms developing in the 19th century include **programme music**, miniature or character pieces, **lieder**, the poetic piano piece and music drama. Musical characteristics of the romantic style include lyricism, expressive chromatic harmony, *rubato* and the development of a larger orchestra. The study of music entitled 'musicology' was also developed during the romantic period.

romanza (It.)
Same as **romance**.

rondeau (Fr.)
A type of medieval French song of the 13th-15th centuries with a choral refrain. This French spelling was used in instrumental works, e.g. by Bach in the baroque period to describe **rondo**.

rondellus

A medieval round of a festive nature composed between 1250 and 1350.

rondeña (Sp.)

A type of **fandango** from Ronda in Andalusia with the unusual harmonies also evident in the **malagueña**.

rondo form

Generally this is an instrumental composition in which one section recurs at certain times. By the 18th century a standard pattern had developed as ABACADA, etc. In Couperin's harpsichord music these sections were detached and rather similar to a formal dance. With later 18th-century composers, e.g. Mozart, the form became common as a more extended piece for the last movement of a sonata or concerto in which sections flowed into one another. The recurring theme A is called the 'rondo theme' and BCD, etc. represent the contrasting sections known as 'episodes'. However, A can be varied. The combination of sonata form and rondo resulting in **sonata rondo** was much used by Mozart and Beethoven.

rota (Lat., 'wheel')

Occasionally this term is used for **round**, e.g. of *Sumer is Icumen in*.

round

A short vocal perpetual canon in which voices enter in turn to sing a melody at the octave or at the same pitch. Examples include *London's Burning, Three Blind Mice* and *Old Abraham Brown*.

round dance

A ring dance. This is a dance in which performers dance round in a circle as opposed to the square dance in which dancers are positioned in a square or rectangle.

rumba

A fast, syncopated and rather suggestive Afro-Cuban dance in 2/4 time and divided into an eight-beat pattern. In the 1930s the rumba became popular in the ballroom and in jazz.

running set

This dance was discovered by the folk music collector, Cecil Sharp (1829-1954), in the Appalachian Mountains of the USA but in fact it is of English origin. An active dance in 4/4 time it has an unvaried refrain which can be played to any tunes. Vaughan Williams' *The Running Set* is an example.

S

saltarello or salterello (It.)

A quick Italian dance in 6/8 time with a characteristic jumping feel to the rhythm similar to the **tarantella**. Examples date from the 14th century, but in the 16th and early 17th centuries it was followed by a **passamezzo**. In Mendelssohn's *Italian Symphony* a saltarello is used in the finale.

samba

A highly syncopated quick Brazilian carnival song dance usually in 2/4 time. The term 'samba' is supposedly derived from the African word for 'belly-bounce'. This dance has a happy-go-lucky nature and is performed in a circle with a standard call and response between the lead singer and chorus. The ballroom version which is slower and more sedate is danced in couples.

sarabande

A slow, stately dance in 3/2 or 3/4 time and one of the standard elements of the suite. Originating in Spain, the sarabande is usually in simple **binary form**. Composers of the sarabande include Bach and Handel.

sardana (Sp.)

A Catalonian national dance performed to pipes and drums. Often in sections with two or six beats to the bar, the sardana has a movement with linked hands similar to the **farandole**.

scat singing

A jazz vocal style in which improvised sounds are performed rather than words, e.g. *bop bop de bop, doo n' de doo*, etc. This style has spilled over into other pop styles especially **rock 'n' roll**. The opening line of Little Richard's song *Tutti Frutti* is the sensational *A bop bop a loom op a bop bop boom!*

scherzo (It., 'joke')
Generally, this is a lively movement, occurring e.g. in a string quartet, sonata or symphony. It was developed by Mozart and Beethoven from the **minuet**. Characteristically, it is in 3/4 time in the form AABA with the B section called 'trio'. The joke element need not be present, but the fast tempo and light mood is maintained. Chopin wrote four independent scherzos for piano.

schottische (Ger. plural, 'Scottish')
A popular 19th-century ballroom dance similar to the polka.

scratching
The mixing of sounds and rhythms of records on two turntables. This style was inspired by **rapping**.

secco (It.)
See **recitative**.

seguidilla (Sp.)
A quick Spanish dance in 3/4 time often accompanied by castanets and similar to the **bolero**. Passages sung by the performers (*coplas*) in short lines are a characteristic of this dance which is still popular in Andalusia today.

sequence
Generally, this is a phrase repeated at a higher or lower interval. If the intervals of the repeated phrase are modified to prevent a key change, then this is known as a *tonal sequence*. If the intervals of the repeated phrase are exact and unaltered, then it is a *real sequence*. A sequence may also be a hymn-like composition sung during a Roman Catholic requiem mass or high mass with a non-biblical text.

serenade
A vague term with two meanings. (1) An evening love song performed in the open-air accompanied by a mandolin or guitar to woo a girl. (2) Evening entertainment (especially in the 18th century) in a set of instrumental movements for chamber orchestra or wind group similar to the **divertimento**. The German equivalent is **nachtmusik**, e.g. Mozart's *Eine Kleine Nachtmusik*.

serenata (It.)
An 18th-century title for a secular cantata or short opera, e.g. Handel's *Acis and Galatea*.

serial music, serialism

A 20th-century concept also variously known as *twelve-tone music* (American), *twelve-note music* (British) and *dodecaphonic music*. Originally this style was devised by composers Hauer and Schönberg around 1920. Usually serial music is associated with Schönberg whose first compositions in this style were *Five Piano Pieces op. 23* written between 1920 and 1923. A twelve-note theme is fixed upon with each note used once. This is known as the 'tone-row' or 'series'. Thereafter, it can appear in four main ways: (1) forwards, (2) backwards (or *retrograde*), (3) upside down (*inversion*) and (4) upside down and backwards (*retrograde inversion*). The series can appear and begin on any one of the twelve pitches and more than one note of the series can be used to form a chord. However, serialism mostly forms the basis of a musical work and only Webern's music is truly serial. Schönberg's most important work in this style is *Moses and Aaron*. Berg was another composer in this style.

sevillana (Sp.)

A quick Spanish dance originating in Seville. It is said to be the local type of **seguidilla**.

shanty

A sailors' work song with solo verse (often of an experimental nature) and chorus matching certain rhythmical movements, e.g. pulling a rope together. Examples include *Bobbie Shaftoe* and *Blow the Man Down*.

shimmy

A popular 1920s American dance in **ragtime** style with two beats to the bar. Hindemith's *Piano Suite '1922', op. 26* has a movement in this style.

siciliano (It.), **sicilienne** (Fr.)

A Sicilian dance popular in the baroque period in slow 6/8 or 12/8 time. It is written in the minor key and appears in instrumental music and arias.

simple binary

Same as **binary**.

simple ternary

Same as **ternary**.

sinfonia (It., 'symphony')

In the baroque era this term described an instrumental piece, but later came to mean a prelude, operatic overture, cantata or suite. However, nowadays small orchestras perform under this name. The *sinfonia concertante* (It.) was Mozart's preferred term to 'concerto' for an orchestral work with more than one solo part with less formal display than a solo concerto.

sinfonietta (It.)

A shorter lighter symphony. Sometimes it is used as a performing name for small orchestras.

singspiel (Ger.)

A play with singing. Generally the singspiel is a comic opera with spoken dialogue in the local dialect instead of recitative. In the mid-18th century the singspiel copied the English ballad opera style, but with Mozart it developed independently. Examples include *Die Entführung* (1782) and *The Magic Flute* (1791). In the early 19th century the style combined with German romantic opera and later came to be known simply as German musical comedy.

ska

African and Carribbean music with a combination of R&B and *mento* (local Jamaican dance music) with a polka nature and a heavy bass line. Ska has a shuffle rhythm close to both these styles. In the 1950s and early 1960s the music had a great emphasis on the off-beats and was played with dominant rough-sounding horns, rhythm guitars and drums in a manic style. Ska also developed its own dance, called ska which involved jerky movements of the upper body bowing forward and back while the knees bend and flex with the hands fanning out. This new beat in Britain, however became known as **bluebeat** and performers included Byron Lee and Prince Buster. Ska subsequently slowed down, developing into **rock-steady** and then into **reggae** in the mid-1960s.

skiffle

A British 1950s style originating with jazz traditionalists attempting to revive American country blues roots. Lonnie Donegan, also a jazz player, made skiffle famous and inspired youngsters like John Lennon to form their own skiffle bands. Skiffle was loose, rhythmic and energetic. Ordinary everyday lyrics were accompanied by acoustic guitar (usually playing only three chords), a 'tea-chest bass' and washboard. With Donegan's *Rock Island Line* hitting the British and American charts in 1956, skiffle groups appeared all over the (country competing with the American rock 'n' roll craze. Other hit skiffle singles include *Does Your Chewing Gum Lose its Flavour on the Bedpost Overnight* and *My Old Man's a Dustman* which reached number one in the charts in 1960.

soca

A modern West Indian sound using electric instruments. The term is derived from joining the words 'soul' and 'calypso' together. Characteristics of the style are dance rhythms and repeated lyrics which often reflect social conditions and act as a newspaper. Soca is also heavily amplified and consists of a trap drum set, electric piano or rhythm guitar, bass guitar, synthesiser, horn section, a pair of bongos and two female backing vocals. Soca is always played at local 'jump ups' and at Carnival time.

soleá

An Andalusian folk song in three-line stanzas with assonance between the final syllables of the 1st and 3rd lines.

sonata

Originally, any composition for a single instrument or for one or more solo instruments accompanied by a **continuo**. There was also no strict form. After 1750 (i.e. from the classical period onwards) the sonata became a three- or four-movement work for a solo instrument or a solo instrument with piano accompaniment. A similar work for three instruments (usually two violins and a 'cello) is called a *trio sonata*. A *violin sonata* or *'cello sonata*, etc. always implies a piano accompaniment. A feature of the sonata was the form of the first movement now called **sonata form**. Forerunner examples of this standard form were D. Scarlatti's short one-movement keyboard works (now usually called sonatas) and the compositions of C.P.E. Bach which greatly influenced the Haydn/Mozart sonata. Mozart developed the scheme of having three contrasting movements in a sonata with the first movement (usually an *allegro*) in sonata form. This scheme was continued by Beethoven who sometimes included a **scherzo**.

sonata da camera (It.) or **chamber sonata**

A 17th- and early 18th-century **sonata** for an instrumental ensemble. These works were usually scored for strings with a keyboard background and consisted of several contrasting movements resembling dances from a **suite**, preceded by a **prelude**. At this point the restrictions of having only one or two players in the sonata had not yet arisen. Corelli (1653-1713) composed many works in this style.

sonata da chiesa (It., 'church sonata')

A style similar to the **sonata da camera**, consisting of several movements but of a much graver nature, avoiding the light dance movements. Mostly written for trio sonatas, Corelli's examples have four contrasting movements, slow—fast—slow—fast. However, the number of movements varied until 1750, although the four-movement scheme was used by Bach and Handel.

sonata form, **first movement form** or **compound binary form**

A structure commonly used (since 1750) for a first movement and sometimes the slow and finale movements of a sonata, quartet, symphony or entire overture. The form is divided into three distinct sections: *exposition, development* and *recapitulation* which are sometimes preceded by a slow introduction. The *exposition* consists of the 'first subject' which is a musical idea usually forming the basis of the movement. The first subject is initially stated in the key of the movement. A contrasting 'second subject' or second theme then appears in the dominant or relative major key after a 'transition' or 'bridge-passage' which leads the listener from the first subject into the second. Thereafter, a 'closing theme' appears, sometimes consisting of first subject material, which is brought to an end with a **codetta**. The *development* section expands upon exposition material. A popular technique is to present the first subject in different ways using the transition to bind the section. The development provides a creative test for the composer. The *recapitulation* again presents the exposition, but not as an exact repetition since the exposition has now been influenced by the development section. The composer also at this point wants to heighten the effect of past themes for dramatic purposes as he draws to a close. The second subject must now also be presented in the tonic key which changes the key of the previous transitions and the codetta now develops into a **coda**. Sonata form is ideal for a large scale musical work since it is built upon small themes, has many sections and contrasts of keys, moods, dynamics and provides room for development. Occasionally in slow movements the development section is missed out (*modified sonata form*).

sonata rondo form
This is a combination of **sonata form** and **rondo form**. The five sections involved in rondo form are ABACA. In sonata rondo form, these become ABACAB plus coda in which A becomes the first subject, B the second subject and C the development section. This form was much used by Beethoven.

sonatina, **sonatine** (It., Fr., 'little sonata')
A shorter and lighter **sonata** which is easier to play.

song cycle
A set of songs performed in its entirety and set to words by a single poet. The first example is Beethoven's *An die Ferne Geliebte*. However, in the romantic era Schubert and Schumann used traditional German popular song combined with imaginative accompaniment to illuminate and interpret words. Examples include Schubert's *Winterreise* (Winter Journey) written in 1828 and Schumann's *Frauenliebe und Leben* (A Woman's Life and Loves) written in 1840. Schumann's work has a more interdependent piano part which is more intimate and often has the last say.

soul
An American rock style combination of black gospel music and raunchy R&B club and bar music. Out of the Tamla Motown record company (Detroit) came Sam Cooke a former gospel singer who became a model for soul stars. James Brown also arrived in 1956 with an aggressive individualistic stage approach giving power to soul as dance music. The Memphis Stax label was more commercial and had a characteristic sound: the instrumental work of the Mar-Keys group rhythm and horn sections used in call and response style rather like a chorus. Otis Redding introduced improvisation on lyrics and melodies at the emotional moments in a song. Other Stax artists included Wilson Picket (who recorded a version of *Hey Jude*), Rufus Thomas and Eddie Floyd. Closely connected to the Stax label was Atlantic which produced Aretha Franklin (previously a gospel singer) who came into soul in 1960. Tired of the

night-club circuit she sang gospel-style material never before heard in the charts, e.g. *Natural Woman* and *Chain of Fools* both of 1967. Soul lyrics at this time expressed the feelings of black society and the music became a symbol of power. After 1967 **motown** became more relaxed and performers like The Jackson Five, Smokey Robinson and Marvin Gaye began to have more control over their outputs. Other soul stars included Sly and the Family Stone, Curtis Mayfield and the Delfonics.

sousedskà
A slow Bohemian round dance with three beats to the bar.

spagniletto, spagnoletta, spagniletta, spagnicoletta
An old Italian round dance in which clapping is featured. The term is also found in Elizabethan virginal music in 3 or 4 time.

spiritual
A type of religious American Negro folk song with a call and response style pattern, popular in the 19th century. Characteristics include the use of the pentatonic scale, syncopated rhythms and hymn-like harmonies close to those of the early Baptists and Methodists.

sprechgesang (Ger., 'speech song')
Voice delivery midway between song and speech. Sprechgesang first appeared in Humperdinck's opera *Königskinder* in 1897. The style was mostly used by Schönberg, although he preferred the terms 'sprechstimme' (speaking voice), 'sprechmelodie' (speech melody) or 'rezitation'. An 'x' on the note stem has become the standard indication on the score that sprechgesang is to be used, e.g. in Schönberg's *Die Glückliche Hand* and *Pierrot Lunaire*. However, in performance this is still unclear. For example, in *Pierrot Lunaire* Schönberg directs the voice to 'give a pitch exactly, but then immediately leave it in a fall or rise'. In his *Ode to Napoleon* and *A Survivor from Warsaw*, the notation is simplified by using a one-line staff so that the pitch level can be chosen by the performer. Berg's opera *Wozzeck* introduced a 'half-sung' style of singing midway between song and sprechgesang, and Boulez in *Le Visage Nuptial* introduced a delivery between sprechgesang and speech by directing 'spoken intonation at the indicated pitch'.

square dance
A dance in which perfomers dance in a rectangle or square, as opposed to a round dance which is danced in a circle.

stile rappresentativo (It.)
An early 17th-century term mainly used by opera and oratorio composers when referring to the new and dramatic **recitative**.

stornello (It.)
A type of traditional Tuscan folk song of an improvisatory nature in three-line stanzas.

strathspey
A Scottish dance related to the reel with a slower tempo and 4 beats to the bar. This dance is named after the Scottish Highland region of Strathspey.

stretto (It., 'close and drawn together')
In a musical sense this is an overlapping effect of the entries, e.g. in a fugue in which the entries appear after shorter intervals than they did originally. A *stretto maestrale* occurs when an entire entry or voice is subject to overlapping.

strict canon
See **canon**.

strict counterpoint
See **counterpoint**.

stride
A jazz piano style involving the rhythmic principles of **ragtime**, a strong bass line, an embellished melody and the use of dynamics. James P. Johnson started this style which was influenced by Jelly Roll Morton and Eubie Blake (who wrote *I'm Just Wild About Harry*). In turn Johnson influenced 'Fats' Waller who injected a more sensitive touch to stride piano. Waller's most famous songs included *Ain't Misbehavin'* (1929) and *Honeysuckle Rose* (1934).

strophic
A song in several verses all set to the same music.

sturm und drang (Ger., 'storm and stress')
A powerful romantic expressiveness sweeping Austrian and German music in the 1760s-70s. This style was especially evident in Haydn's symphonies of that time.

style galant (Fr.), **galanter stil** (Ger.)
The musical equivalent of the rococo style in architecture. The

term described the homophonic but ornamented French and Italian music of composers such as F. Couperin and D. Scarlatti, as opposed to the German contrapuntal style. The period of this style (1730-1770) marked an overlapping of **baroque** and early **classical music**.

suite (Fr., 'a following')

Originally, an instrumental composition consisting of a group of dance movements all in the same key. In the 17th century the German composer Froberger wrote suites in the order of **allemande, courante** and **sarabande**, with possibly a **gigue** after the allemande or courante. However, in 1693 these suites were published in the order allemande, courante, sarabande, gigue and this was the order adopted by Handel and Bach. Often Bach's suites have other French dance types, e.g. **bourrée, gavotte, minuet** or **passepied** and his *English Suites* have a prelude. These dances were in the characteristic **binary form** which in the mid-18th century, developed into **sonata form**. The suite having been the dominating instrumental form was also succeeded by the **sonata** and the **symphony**. A suite may also describe a set of movements arranged from a ballet or opera score.

swing

A jazz style mainly performed by big-bands and dating from around 1930 when the roots of jazz (**ragtime** and **blues**) merged with the blues-riff bands of the north. Swing was a truly popular and cosmopolitan music style with the compelling ingredients of elusive but also hesitating rhythms which could not easily be notated. In the early jazz days big-bands consisted of eight or nine pieces. By the late 1920s, these had increased to 13 or 16 with which we now associate the style. The bigger band offered more authority of tone, stronger compelling riffs and the mixing of modes, e.g. combining 'hot jazz' (usually in the form of soloists) with 'sweet jazz' (represented in the mellower reed and brass sections). The saxophone was an integral part of swing which was uncommon in previous jazz groups. Although soloists like Benny Goodman (clarinettist) and Lester Young (saxophonist) emerged from the swing era, arrangers like Glen Miller were of great importance creating unique sounds and versions of popular songs. Other swing greats include Count Basie, Coleman Hawkins, Duke Ellington and Earl Hines.

symbolism

A poetic movement in literature closely related to **impressionism** in music which reacted against the strong feelings of the romantic writers like Hugo. Symbolist poets included Mallarmé and Baudelaire. Debussy was influenced by the poets Mallarmé and Verlaine and his composition *Prélude à l'apres-midi d'un faune* (1892) evoked Mallarmé's poem.

symphonic dance

A serious orchestral piece with a dance-like rhythm and nature.

symphonic poem

Otherwise known as **programme music** or **tone-poem**, this is a mid-19th-century term introduced by Liszt to describe an orchestral piece influenced by literature, art or emotions. Liszt realised that a one-movement work free from sonata form or the formal structure of the whole symphony would enable a more accurate representation of the subject. To represent ideas or personalities in his music Liszt employed a device he entitled the 'metamorphosis of themes'. As the music progressed and moods and characters changed, so the themes were developed and altered. This idea was closely connected to Berlioz' **idée fixe** and Wagner's **leitmotif**. Other composers writing in this style included Smetana, Franck, Sibelius, Dukas and Strauss.

symphony

Generally a four-movement orchestral work involving a first movement, a second movement, minuet and trio and a finale. The first movement is often in **sonata form**, but this may also be the structure for other movements especially the slow movement and the finale. The symphony developed from other orchestral forms during the transition between the baroque and classical eras. These forms were chiefly the Italian overture (or **sinfonia**) favoured by A. Scarlatti in fast—slow—fast form, the **concerto grosso** movements marked with dynamics, the suite from which the minuet and trio is taken and **opera buffa** which is represented in the early witty style of writing. C.P.E. Bach, Gluck and Stamitz (of the Mannheim school, notable for the use of dynamics) were significant composers of early symphonies. The four-movement form became standard about 1760 in the works of Haydn and also Mozart. Haydn's twelve *London* Symphonies represent a culmination of output with a large classical orchestra consisting of pairs of flutes, oboes, clarinets, bassoons, horns (sometimes more since they were much favoured), trumpets, timpani and strings. Beethoven increased the orchestra further in his symphonies, writing more technically difficult parts. His symphonies present a unity of mood, sometimes by a joining of movements, e.g. the last two in his *Fifth Symphony*. Other great symphonic composers include Mahler (who used the human voice), Schubert, Sibelius and Nielson. Beethoven's tendency towards a narrative programme in his *Sixth Symphony* influenced Berlioz' *Romeo and Juliette* (a 'dramatic symphony') and Liszt's symphonic poems. Modern composers of symphonies employing a flexible number of movements include Vaughan Williams, Prokofiev, Shostakovich, Hindemith Stravinsky and Tippett.

syncopation
A term describing the emphasis placed on the off-beat. Characteristic of jazz styles, e.g. **ragtime**.

system of Glareanus
Glareanus was the pseudonym of Loriti (1488-1563), a Swiss theorist who argued in his treatise *Dodecachordon* (1597) that there were twelve not eight church modes. These four additional modes were the Aeolian and Hypoaeolian (with final on A) and Ionian and Hypoionian (with final on C). See **modes**.

T

tafelmusik (Ger.), **musique de table** (Fr.), **table music**
Music composed in medieval times, especially for a banquet. The term is also applied to Telemann's long, light suites.

taleadas (Sp.)
A vigorous type of **seguidilla**, influenced by the **cachucha**.

tango
An Argentine dance in moderately slow 2/4 time with syncopated rhythms. Appeared in European and US ballrooms around World War I. The tango was stylised by Stravinsky in his *Histoire du Soldat* (1917).

tarantella (It.)
A fast Italian dance with alternating major and minor key sections in 6/8 time. The dance takes its name from Taranto in southern Italy where the tarantula spider is found. This dance was said to cure a bite from this dreaded spider.

tattoo
Army music of bugles and drums, originally recalling soldiers to their barracks at night. Lasting 20 minutes in the British Army, it begins with the 'first post' and ends with the 'last post', with the latter often being heard as the conclusion of a military funeral. The Edinburgh Military Tattoo, held during August-September, is a two-hour outdoor spectacle consisting of military pipes and drums, brass bands, dancing and displays of military expertise involving performers from across the world.

ternary form
A composition in three sections in the form ABA. The first section (A) is repeated (not necessarily exactly) and (B) represents a different middle section. The title may also describe

the conventional 'minuet and trio' form in which (A) is initially stated twice (AABA). If the restatement is unchanged (ABA), it is often indicated by 'da capo al fine' at the end of the middle section as it would be in a 'da capo aria' or minuet with trio. If the statement is abbreviated, the indication is 'dal segno al fine'. Romantic short piano pieces such as nocturnes and rhapsodies are often in this form. **Sonata form** is also a type of ternary form.

theme
A melodic group of notes forming the basis or chief idea in a composition by its repetition and development. In musical analysis the theme is equated with 'subject', but it can also be applied to recognisable elements within a subject. In 'theme and variations' the term describes a long musical subject which is developed. Liszt's term for a theme's changing and varying to suit dramatic purposes in his **symphonic poems** is the 'metamorphosis of themes'.

thorough bass
See **basso continuo**.

tin pan alley
Popular commercial music of the early 20th century. The expression is derived from the untuneful sounds made by hard-at-work New York commercial song-writers who were not great pianists. The noise was described by a musician ,passing through West 28th Street, as sounding like 'tin pans'. Tin pan alley was commercial music with three main ingredients for songs. They had to be (1) written in a fashionable musical style (2) be socially aware and (3) appeal to the public's emotions. Commercial value was, however, of greatest importance. One of the styles emerging from tin pan alley was the sentimental ballad. Examples of songs in this style include *Yes, We Have No Bananas* and *Tea for Two*.

tirana (Sp.)
An Andalusian popular song-dance.

toccata (It., *toccare,* to touch)
This is generally a solo instrumental piece involving rapid changes of notes to demonstrate the player's touch. Often the toccata is followed by a fugue, e.g. the famous *Toccata and Fugue in D minor* by Bach. Towards the end of the 16th century two types

were written. Frescobaldi and A. and G. Gabrieli wrote in a free style with considerable passage work. Merulo (and later Frescobaldi) wrote in section but also in a free style. Other composers of toccatas were Froberger, Pachelbel and Buxtehude (whom Bach greatly admired). However, the term was also applied around 1600 to a short composition for brass of a fanfare nature.

trescone

A rapid and lively popular folk dance of Florence. The dance is in duple time and involves the throwing of handkerchiefs in the air.

triple concerto

A concerto for three soloists with orchestra, e.g. Beethoven's op. 56 for piano, violin, 'cello and orchestra written in 1805.

twist

A 1960s dance craze influenced by the rock 'n' roll spirit of the 1950s. The television rock show, *American Bandstand* promoted the twist, with Chubby Checker reaching number one in the charts with a cover version of *The Twist*. Other twist hits included Bill Doggett's *Let's Do the Hully Gully Twist*, Rod Mckuen's *The Oliver Twist* and Santo and Johnny's *Twistin' Bells*.

two-tone

A late 1970s and early 1980s style dedicated to dance-floor music involving racially mixed bands with **reggae** roots. Examples of two-tone bands include The Specials who sang *Gangsters* (1979) and *Ghost Town* (1981), Madness, Bad Manners and The Bodysnatchers.

U

utility music
see **gebrauchmusik**.

underground rock
A mid- to late 1960s psychedelic-based music style of an experimental and improvisational nature. The underground rock movement was the soul of the hippie movement and involved sound and light shows (influenced by the San Francisco psychedelic scene), poetry readings, films and acting. The first underground club UFO (Unlimited Freak Out in underground terms) was organised by John Hopkins. Disc jockey John Peel and *It* music journalist Miles were instrumental in pioneering the British scene. An event which characterised the philosophies of the underground clubs was the 14-hour Technicolour Dream held in April, 1967 at Alexandra Palace. Attracting over 5,000 hippies, it featured many underground groups in Britain, e.g. Pink Floyd, Soft Machine, The Social Deviants, Purple Gang, The Bonzo Dog Doodah Band and The Crazy World of Arthur Brown. Folk and jazz groups were also evident in the underground, e.g. Pentangle which blended folk, blues, jazz and 'classical music', and Fairport Convention which played arrangements of American writers like Leonard Cohen and Joni Mitchell. Bob Dylan also influenced the underground. The improvisational quality of underground music began to be influenced by composers like Messiaen, Varèse, Satie and Stravinsky. Jazz players like Ornette Coleman and John Coltrane also influenced rock music of this time. The underground faded out in 1968.

V

vamping

A piano style of playing which extemporises around three simple key chords to accompany a singer etc. Vamping books are sold dealing with three main chords in a key, e.g. I, II and V.

vaudeville

Originally, an early 18th-century satirical Paris street song of topical content. Later it came to mean a final song in entertainment with verses sung by different characters in turn, e.g. in Mozart's *Die Entführung* composed in 1782. In the 19th century the term was applied to music hall comedies interspersed with songs. Nowadays it describes variety entertainment.

verbunko

A late 18th- and early 19th-century Hungarian military dance. The dance however, was set to gypsy music in the form of a slow introduction, the *lassú*, followed by a quick section, the *friss*. Liszt and Bartok used this structure in their Hungarian Rhapsodies and it also became popular in the theatre. The verbunko is similar to the **csárdás**.

villancico (Sp. *villano,* 'rustic')

A popular but sophisticated song of the late 15th and early 16th centuries. It begins with a refrain which is repeated after each verse. In the 17th and 18th centuries the term referred to a Christmas cantata for soloists and chorus. In modern Spanish, a villancico is a Christmas carol.

villanella (It.)

A Neapolitan madrigal of a light-hearted and less contrapuntal nature popular in the 16th century. It had a simple rhythmic structure and the music was repeated for many verses. The use of consecutive fifths was a feature.

volta (It.)
A lively dance in 6/8 time popular in the late 16th and early 17th centuries. A characteristic of the dance was the swinging of the women high in the air by the men. The dance is also known as 'lavolta', both words meaning 'time' in Italian, e.g. 'prima volta', first time.

voluntary
Generally this is a keyboard piece in free style written especially for organ. The term often refers to an organ solo played at the beginning and ending of a church service.

W

waltz, valse (Fr.), **walzer** (Ger.), **valzer** (It.)
A slow or fast dance in triple time with the characteristic one beat and one chord in the bar. The waltz became universally popular in the 19th century through the Viennese composer Lanner and the Strauss family. *The Blue Danube* (1867) was written by the young Johann Strauss.

Y

yodel
English spelling of **jodel**.

Z

zapateado (Sp.)
A rigorous Spanish clog-dance in triple time with an aggressive rhythm. A characteristic is the stamping of feet as opposed to the usual clicking of the Spanish castanets.

zarzuela (Sp.)
The traditional one-act Spanish operetta with spoken dialogue, songs and choruses. It is often of a satirical nature. A famous example of a zarzuela is Valverde's *La Gran Via* (The High Road) of 1886.

zortziko
A Basque folk dance with 5 beats to the bar and with the 2nd and 4th beats written as dotted notes.

zwischenspiel (Ger., 'between-play')
Music of an interlude or intermezzo nature. The term is mostly applied to organ playing between hymn stanzas, fugue episodes or solo sections between concerto 'tutti'.